The B♥R♥I♥D♥E♥S Wedding Guide: Help Me Find a Wedding Dress

I0093405

Rosanna Haller

Celestial
Publishing

Copyright © 2013 Rosanna Haller

All rights reserved worldwide. No part of this publication may be replicated, reproduced, redistributed, or given away in any form without prior permission, in writing from the author or the publisher, Celestial Publishing, 1818 W. Francis Ave. Suite 202, Spokane, WA 99205, USA.

ISBN-13: 978-1-60655-004-5

Printed in the United States of America

To YOU; The Bride!

You deserve to look and feel your best on your wedding day. You deserve to find a gown that you LOVE. Your wedding day is YOUR red carpet moment. It's exciting!

So how do you find the perfect wedding dress for you?

Simply follow the 6 proven, easy to follow, step-by-step elements every bride should consider when choosing her wedding gown. These pages are crammed with beautiful photos and illustrations that show you what you need to know.

The B.R.I.D.E.S. Wedding Guide will help transform you from a bewildered bride into a savvy shopper.

Here's to the Wedding Dress of Your Dreams!

♥ *ROSANNA*

CONTENTS

Component Parts of a Wedding Dress

Wedding Planning Tips

Wedding Planning Tips (continued)

How to Find

MY WEDDING DRESS

Your wedding dress may be one of the most important clothing purchases of your life, because your wedding gown will set the tone, look, and feel of your entire wedding. No matter what your vision is for your wedding, this is your chance to be in the spotlight. This is your "red-carpet" moment. All eyes will be on you!

Your wedding gown should reflect you (at your core) while still taking into consideration when and where your wedding will take place, how formal your wedding will be, and most of all it should look and feel picture-perfect when it's on you!

It's likely you had some indication that this day was coming. Perhaps you've already been looking through bridal magazines, watching bridal shows, and looking in store windows. You know your general size and figure considerations. You may have some idea of the dress you'd like to find.

The B♥R♥I♥D♥E♥S Process

Use the B♥R♥I♥D♥E♥S process to help you find your wedding dress. Some parts of the process will be more important to you, and some lesser, but make sure you consider each step.

First you'll want a wedding gown that best compliments your unique Body Type. You will discover which wedding dress silhouettes, necklines, waistlines and more will be most attractive on you.

This guide has *over 200 detailed custom illustrations* so you can see and learn what different wedding dress terms mean. You will find hints and tips with each illustration that explains which gowns will be the most beautiful on you. You'll feel more confident when you walk into a bridal boutique with a clear understanding of what type of wedding dress you desire, and the proper name to call it.

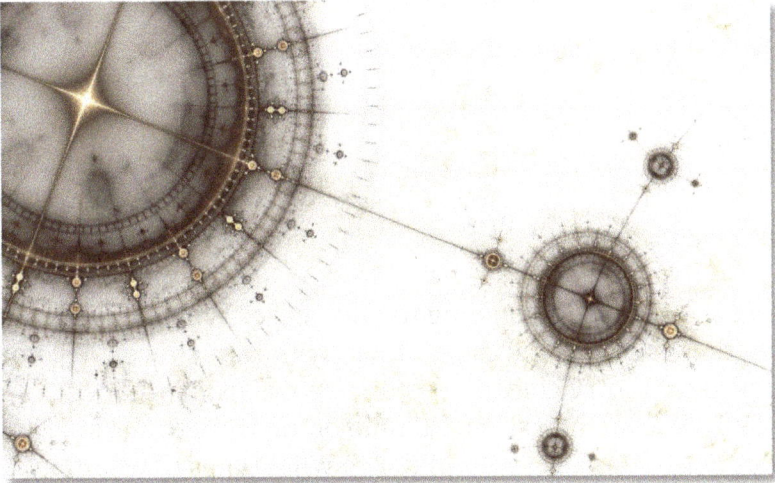

The next point to consider when choosing your wedding dress is your **Religion**; your own moral compass. We all have our own deeply rooted beliefs of right and wrong. You may feel great in a mini skirt, or you may need a dress with sleeves. If you attend a specific church, or belong to a particular religion, they may have dress criteria to which you should adhere. If not, you will have your own standards of dress. Stick to them.

The next element is your personality at its core. What is it that makes you uniquely you? What is your beauty style? From princess to glam girl, from Victorian to preppy, expressing your **Individuality** through the choice of your wedding gown is most important. This is why, though a wedding dress may fit, it may not fit *you*.

Where is your wedding going to take place? Will you walk down the aisle in a church, or stand by the sea shore? Will you marry in a country club, or exchange vows in an outdoor garden? Will you marry in a temple or on a hill top? Your wedding **Destination** will influence what types of wedding gowns are suitable.

Black tie to creative, how formal your wedding **Event** will be will determine if your wedding dress of choice is suitable for the occasion.

When are you being married? The **Season** of your wedding will affect your fabric choices.

Stay Calm. With research, planning, patience and the help of this guide, you'll find the dress you love. Let's get started...

Body Type

I AM ONE-OF-A-KIND

As you embark on your journey to find that *UNIQUE* wedding dress design that enhances all that is lovable about *YOU*, you might discover that you are uniquely you and don't fit into any standard mold. Designers have tried to standardize sizes but the dress form size 6 has changed so much over the years that it's nearly impossible to know what your 'real' size is.

Today however it is all about **you** and finding the wedding dress that is ideal for **your** unique body type. Each of us is unique. Take a look at your actual shape to help determine the best dress style for you *without regard* to size number.

What looks divine in a magazine or on someone else might be inappropriate for your physique. You'll be your best self when you balance your headpiece, embellishments, and dress shape to the figure you have.

Body Type

There are many ways to label various figure types. You may find you fall somewhere in between.

Consider the bulk (flesh) distribution around your skeletal frame; for example, large back and small bust; large bust and small back; wide flat front waist and rounded protruding bottom; large hip and flat stomach; protruding stomach and flat rear.

In this list, some descriptions overlap, or you may see yourself in two or more types, such as petite but curvy.

APPLE: Rounder and fuller at the top and middle than at the bottom with little back curve; not narrow hipped; sometimes with a larger belly.

> Draw attention to the shoulders and floor with a strapless mermaid.

ATHLETIC: More angular feminine shaped curves.

> Add softness and curves with a full skirt and Basque waist.

SMALL BUST: Bust that measures more than 2" less than the hips with most of the weight in the back.

> Try sweetheart necklines with beading or surplice wrap folds, ruching, or draping; wide straps, wide necklines, neckline insets.

CURVY: Proportionate features that are soft and full, of any size.

> For proportionate girls, anything goes.

HOURGLASS: Bust and hips are approximately the same size with a waist that measures at least 2" less; a ratio or 10-12" differences between the bust, waist, and hips.

> For you, anything goes.

INVERTED TRIANGLE: Proportionate body of any size; shoulders are obviously wider than the hips.

> Balance hips with a full mermaid or A-line style, V- or U-necks. Keep shoulder embellishments to a minimum.

LARGE BUST: Bust that measures more than 2" larger than the hips, with most of the weight in the front, not in the back.

> A-lines, full skirts, asymmetrical lines at the lower body will elongate you and draw some of the attention down.

FULL FIGURED: Soft full features but on a larger scale, usually proportionate.

> Proportionate figures can wear any style; vertical and diagonal lines slenderize.

PEAR SHAPE: The circumference of the hips is about 4" or larger than the circumference of the bust, with a waist not larger than the hips and often with narrow shoulders.

> Upper body embellishments and horizontal lines at the upper body, full sleeves, wide necklines, vertical or asymmetrical lines at the lower body.

PLUS SIZE: Larger overall, of any size, either soft and usually without a defined waist, or angular and defined.

> A-lines to soften the waist and camouflage hips, illusion inset at neckline, vertical or asymmetrical lines from draping or beading.

LINEAR: A straighter line at the sides of the body, having a less defined waist; sometimes referred to as rectangular.

Add curves and fullness with A-line skirts, embellished bodices, sweetheart or rounded necklines, full skirts, draping, and asymmetrical folds, or ruching.

LONG TORSO: The upper portion of the body is longer than the legs, measuring more than 3x the length of the head. The head is used to measure key points of the body. (Where head length is used, measure from the top of the crown to chin level. Of course, this assumes perfect proportions. Even your head may be somewhat smaller or larger, so use your best judgment.)

Keep the waistline at the natural waist or above, raised waist styles, wide waistband, empire, inverted Basque.

SHORT TORSO: The upper portion of the body is shorter than the legs, measuring less than 3x the length of the head.

Drop waist styles, Basque waist.

SHORT WAIST: The distance between the bottom of the ribs and the hip bone is less than the length of the head.

A-lines and drop waist styles, Basque waist, diagonal or vertical lines from ruching or draping.

LONG WAIST: The distance between the bottom of the ribs and the hip bone is more than the length of the head.

Keep the waist seam at the natural waist, raised waist styles, wide waistband, inverted Basque, full skirts.

PETITE: Approximately 5'3" and under, of any shape or size.

Strapless styles, dropped waists, vertical lines, and embellishments proportionate to your height.

THIN: Little padding, with our without curves.

A-lines with wide necklines, ruching, draping, tiers, hip flowers, and puff sleeves will make you appear fuller.

THICK: Linear but not thin or slim.

To create curves, try A-line or full skirted styles, wide curved necklines.

WILLOWY: Usually taller than 5'6" with less padding but otherwise proportionate.

> You can wear any style. Waist seams at the natural waist will cut your visual height.

PREGNANT: This body will change rapidly, gaining a larger middle, rear, bust, hip, and even feet.

> Simple is best; Columns, empires, fuller sleeves will draw the eye up, V-necks.

Here are some tips to help you balance your figure:

TO WIDEN NARROW SHOULDERS OR UPPER BODY:
Off-shoulder styles, wide collars and necklines, horizontal detailing, puff sleeves, strapless styles.

TO WIDEN HIPS AND BALANCE A WIDER SHOULDER:
Dropped waists with the waist seem at the hip, any embellishment at the hip such as ruching, draping, florals, or flounces; mermaid or full skirt styles.

TO ENHANCE A SMALLER BUST: Ruching or draping, wide keyholes, surplice bodice, wide straps to add bulk, and neckline insets.

TO BALANCE A LARGER BUST: A-lines, dropped waists, or mermaid styles, wider straps (instead of spaghetti straps).

TO ACCENT OR CREATE A WAIST: A-lines, any embellishments that will make the shoulders and hips appear wider, asymmetrical lines to draw the eye away from the waist.

IF YOU'RE PREGNANT: Try empire waists or columns to enhance the belly; a more busy upper bodice and full lower skirt to draw the eye away from it.

TO CREATE CURVES: A-line or surplice styles, sweetheart or rounded necklines, and asymmetrical draping, full skirts.

TO DIMINISH HEIGHT: Waist seams at the natural waist, horizontal lines, shorter hem lengths.

TO ADD VISUAL HEIGHT: Dropped waist styles, floor length styles, neckline inset to carry the eye all the way up, vertical or asymmetrical lines.

Once you have decided on the basic wedding dress design for your body shape, you can get creative with details like fabric, sleeves, waistlines, or skirt types and lengths. Adding embellishments like lace and beads can create a more or less formal dress and enhance or hide particular areas of your anatomy.

Religion

MY MORAL COMPASS

Choosing an appropriate style to suit your chosen faith, religious, or moral standards may be at the top of your list when you search for a wedding dress. Take into amount of bare skin you're willing to expose while searching for a wedding dress, or make changes to a dress you love.

Your level of modesty is a result of your beliefs, your upbringing, and your personal taste. A church or temple wedding may require some amount of modesty and specific denominations may have requirements to which you must adhere, but that doesn't mean you need to sacrifice style for the dress of your dreams.

Many styles can be brought into the range of appropriateness with simple modifications or the addition of a jacket or shrug.

If you already have a style in mind that is without issues, you won't have to worry about this, but for those whose idea of the perfect dress needs some tweaking, here are some suggestions:

- If you like a bare look but don't want to expose your arms, wear long sleeves that are made entirely of lace
- For bustier styles, try a lace jacket that buttons in back
- Try a silk bolero style jacket with 3/4 sleeves
- Have a lace inset added to low necklines
- Find dresses with sleeves, or have sleeves added
- Choose a re-embroidered lace bateau neck that continues in one piece to a long lace sleeve
- Opt for narrow V-necks, slits, or keyholes that don't expose cleavage
- Avoid silhouettes that are heavily fitted below the high hip or navel
- Wear hose with any style that exposes your legs, or your feet if you're wearing open-toed shoes or sandals
- For fitted skirts, add ruching, ruffles, or tiers to conceal your figure
- For open back styles, wear an attached lace collar that covers the upper back, and shoulders
- Have wide straps added to a strapless dress
- For low back necklines, add a Watteau that extends from both shoulders
- Choose a veil that covers you face and back and extends over bare shoulders and bust
- Avoid clingy dresses in lightweight fabric

Individuality

MY CORE PERSONALITY

U nlike times past when everything had rules set in place and the boundaries of wedding dress styles fell into just a few categories, today's dresses need to fit in with the overall wedding theme, capture the imagination of the audience, be eye-rollingly stunning, age and climate appropriate, affordable, and fulfill the bride's vision and expectations.

Most people will never plan a large catered event in their lifetimes, except in the case of their wedding. Coordinating the venue with food, desserts and cakes, colors, favors, dresses, linens, vendors including photographers, videographers, musicians, and florists, invitations and thanks you notes, personnel and press photos, can become mind boggling. It's like producing a small film with you creating the story board, hiring the cast and crew, producing, directing, and acting in the leading role. Oh, and yes, you're in charge of costumes, too.

Though trends in dresses come and go, it doesn't matter what's in or what's not in. What *you* want is what counts. So how do you stay sane among all the challenges that go along with planning, *and* get the wedding dress you want without caving in to the pressure?

The theme and the dress should be the first things you think about when you know you're getting married. In fact, most girls have been thinking about these two things long before they're asked for their hand. They have a vision and that vision reflects their innermost self. Making it all come together the way you envision it, however, is something that takes a little coordinated planning.

Know Your Personality

To do this, consider your individuality, your personality, your lifestyle, your preferred fashion style, your favorite colors and the colors which best suit you, and what you consider to be your perfect wedding dress.

Your colors, your beauty scheme, your flowers, your cake, and your venue may all play a part in choosing your gown, but ultimately, the gown is the deciding factor that sets the tone for the rest of the wedding. It reflects all the best of your dreams and artistic vision. Once you've set your style in mind, don't let yourself be talked out of it and into something else. Often friends and relatives have the best intentions, but their vision for you is not your vision. In some cases, they may project their own vision of the perfect dress onto you.

Check your vision against your individual personality here to help you determine what kind of gown will suit you perfectly. Categories will almost always overlap, and in the end, you'll use the process of elimination to determine the best dress style for your personality.

How To Decide

Most of us will fall into more than one category. You'll notice that someone who is artistic, for example, can be romantic, whimsical, nostalgic or traditional. You'll need to keep narrowing it down until you "feel" the right style for you. You'll begin to see a pattern emerge as you see yourself defined by the same adjectives more than a few times. When you start choosing the same adjectives over and over again, you're getting close.

What best describes the gown you think you'll love or the one you've always dreamed about?

STRAPLESS BALL GOWN: princess, fairy tale, romantic, formal, regal

MERMAID SILHOUETTE: Sensual, glamorous, flirty, powerful, striking

HELP ME FIND A WEDDING DRESS

A-LINE WITH MINIMAL EMBELLISHMENT: traditional, conservative, classic , subdued

SIMPLE SILHOUETTE WITH LACE: romantic, traditional

ORNATE BODICE, PUFF SLEEVES: regal, formal, glamorous

GRECIAN, COLUMN: romantic, traditional, historical, conservative, classical, subdued

EMPIRE: romantic, historical, whimsical, nostalgic

HEAVILY EMBELLISHED THROUGHOUT: romantic, historical, artistic, regal

COLORED DRESS ELEMENTS: artistic, romantic, whimsical

HEAVY DRESS FABRICS: powerful, regal

LIGHT DRESS FABRICS: romantic, flirty, subdued

LOTS OF TULLE: romantic, artistic, whimsical, flirty

LOTS OF LACE: romantic, traditional, nostalgic

What's your preferred venue?

Venue sizes, styles and locations can often be made to emulate the theme or style of your wedding, but choosing one that closely matches your vision saves you a lot of time and money on re-doing it to look like what you want.

HOTEL BALLROOM: Traditional, formal, regal

COUNTRY CLUB: preppy, traditional, formal, classic, subdued

RESTAURANT: modern, artistic, classic

GARDEN: romantic, whimsical, artistic, traditional

BEACH: romantic, whimsical, artistic, flirty

TEA HOUSE: romantic, artistic, contemporary, subdued, classic, whimsical

What Flowers do you love?

If you've always liked a certain flower or style of flower, this is a big clue regarding the style of gown that might suit you best.

FLOWERS WITH MANY PETALS; **and tight buds such as roses:** traditional, classic, romantic

LARGE HEAD FLOWERS; **like lilies, tulips, and orchids:** romantic, artistic

SMALL PETAL FLOWERS; **that grow in clusters like lily of the valley, baby's breath, and some trilliums:** whimsical, subdued, nostalgic, romantic, historical

UNIQUE FLOWERS SHAPES LIKE BIRD OF PARADISE: artistic, contemporary, *avant garde.*

What's your beauty style?

Glamour girls love makeup. Some girls never wear makeup. How much, how often, and the style of your makeup indicates your leanings in fashion.

SOFT PINK OR RED LIPSTICK: romantic, flirty

DEEP OR BRIGHT RED LIPSTICK: glamour girl, powerful

MINIMAL BLUSH AND LIP GLOSS: romantic, flirty

EXTRA EYE SHADOW AND BLUSH: artistic

SMOKY EYES WITH LOTS OF LINER AND PALE LIPS: quiet glamour, *avant garde*, contemporary

COLOR ON THE EYES LIKE PURPLE, GREEN OR BLUE: whimsical, artistic, extrovert

DON'T WEAR MAKEUP OR WEAR VERY LITTLE: minimalist, subdued

ALWAYS WEAR LIPSTICK: formal, traditional, glamorous

NEVER WEARS LIPSTICK: preppy, minimalist, tomboy

What are your wedding colors?

What you like is what counts most. If you're partial to certain colors, this may indicate what your dress style should be.

FORMAL: Red, metallic gold, and metallic silver

CONTEMPORARY: Black and white, charcoal and white, all white, and all black

PREPPY: Pinks, yellows, blues, and browns

WHIMSICAL, ARTISTIC: Sunny yellow, oranges, purples, deep pinks, and greens

REGAL: Antique gold, forest green, red, royal purple, royal blue, silver

ROMANTIC: Pinks, reds, non-metallic gold, deep greens, light blues

What's your wedding style?

There are no rules regarding where you have your wedding and many styles will overlap. If you love the idea of a castle wedding, that's a big clue to the kind of dress that will best suit you.

FORMAL: cathedral, church or temple ceremonies, hotels, banquet rooms, country clubs, palaces, mansions, and castles, historical settings

CONTEMPORARY: registry office ceremonies, small venues, tea rooms, breakfast venues, museums, structural arches, boutique hotels

PREPPY: country clubs, sports arenas, college halls

WHIMSICAL: beaches, parks, gardens, amusement venues, tea houses, boutique hotels, natural arches, wooded areas, lodges

REGAL: museums and cultural venues, cathedral, church, and temple ceremonies, banquet halls, formal gardens, palaces, mansions, and castles, historical settings

ROMANTIC: gardens, natural arches, tea rooms, castles, historical settings, wooded areas

What's your personality type?

Clean and Classic: *TRADITIONALIST*

You're traditional in your views and lean toward simple graceful lines.

Look at A-lines with minimal embellishment

Simple lace covered bodices

Raw satin or Dupioni silk shrugs with 3/4 sleeves

Pearl ornamentation instead of stones

Columnar dresses such as sheaths or Grecian styles with one shoulder and a narrow belt

High necklines with keyholes

Bateau, square, and jewel necklines

Whimsical: *FUNKY, FUN, ARTISTIC*

You like to change things up and tend to throw the unexpected into the mix.

Look at empire waist dresses with puff or Juliet sleeves or mermaid styles with colored tulle underneath

Colored embellishments and accessories such as sashes, belts, stones, and ornate fascinators or combine dip-dyed colors with accessories such as yellow dye and a silver belt, black dye and red rosettes, hot pink dye and antique gold tulle crinoline, or green dye with pink stones

Carry a wire spray with gold balls on the ends, starfish, bells, shells, or anything that represents your whimsy, and mix them in with non-traditional flowers or ferns

Tiered skirts that resemble flower petals

Dip-dyed hems or edges of long bell sleeves

Lots of tulle layers in color combinations either as a skirt or under a skirt, such as blue, red, or white mixed with gold, black and pink, red and white, or marigold and silver

Nostalgic: *ROMANTIC, ARTISTIC, TRADITIONAL*

You have a variety of interests ranging from historical storybook romanticism to contemporary mid-century art. Think about your preferred setting to determine the direction you want to take.

Look at princess styles with sweetheart necklines and puff sleeves

Try A-line waists that flare dramatically at the hip topped with a back-buttoning lace jacket

Consider a one shoulder sheath with a wide leather belt and studded buckle

Halter necklines

Portrait collars with A-line skirts

Princess: *ROMANTIC, TRADITIONAL, NOSTALGIC*

The princess gown or full skirted ball gown is one of the most popular choices in wedding dress styles, but real princesses come in many shapes and colors.

Look at *quinceañera* dresses in colors

Tea length dresses with skirts made completely of tulle layers

Tulle layers in colors such as blue and gold, red and white, green and pink, or marigold and white

Scalloped overlays with large satin rosettes at the bustle points

Large puff sleeves

Fur shrugs over strapless bodices

A white, blue, or forest green velvet gown studded with flowers or stones

Velvet empire dress with long fitted sleeves

Basque or inverted Basque waistlines

Glam Girl: *40S, 80S, RETRO, POWER FEMME, RICH GIRL, FLIRTY*

You want control and you want to be noticed.

Look at dresses with lots of embellishment at the top of the dress, near your face

Use bright stones on accessories

Figure hugging styles such as mermaids and corsets

Large or ornate hair ornaments, fascinators or hats

Jeweled headbands or crowns

Preppy: *TRADITIONAL, CONSERVATIVE*

This category usually sticks to a set standard of rules regarding color and style.

Look at structural gowns with square necklines

Eliminate lace

Use pearl embellishment instead of stones

A-line dresses with minimal ornamentation

Solid matte silk jackets with short or 3/4 sleeves instead of lace or fur jackets

Accessory colors in medium shades of green or blue, navy, charcoal, red, wine, russet, or browns

Romantic: *NOSTALGIC, ARTISTIC, TRADITIONAL, CLASSIC, FLIRTY*

A romantic gown can be vintage, modern, beachy , regal, or classical

Don't stick to white if you like color. A romantic fairytale look can be achieved by having the bottom of an A-line gown dip-dyed in pink or antique gold

For a beach venue, have iridescent blue crystals sewn onto your dress in a swirl or wave pattern

Look at softly draped styles such as columns

Larger than life styles such as full skirted ball gowns with large puff sleeves

Empire waists with straight skirts and long Juliet or poet sleeves

Victorian: *ROMANTIC, NOSTALGIC, TRADITIONAL*

Queen Victoria of England started the tradition of wearing a white gown. Prior to her wedding, the expected color was blue as set forth by the Roman Catholic Church.

If you love the Victorian era, look at full skirts with off shoulder bodices

Use lots of lace everywhere

Wear an enameled or stone encrusted bird pin that suits your personality and give one to each of your bridesmaids the way Queen Victoria did

Wear your hair in a low roll at the nape of the neck and a floral wreath that starts under the roll

If you use any color, make it blue and keep it to a minimum

Fairytale Queen: *WHIMSICAL, ARTISTIC, GLAMOROUS, POWERFUL*

This is different than the princess in that the queen is bolder, less romantic in the sense of storybook characters.

Look at mermaid styles with lots of embellishment top and bottom

Bodices with lots of embellishment and straight or columnar skirts

Long fitted sleeves without lace or ruffles

Heavier fabrics such as velvet embellished with colored stones

Brocade with wide pleated detail at the hem

Large portrait and Queen Anne style collars

Wide square necklines

Bold colors such as red, midnight blue, forest green, black, antique gold, metallic silver, and metallic copper

Subdued: *TRADITIONAL, ROMANTIC, CLASSIC*

You know what you want but don't like to be loud about it.

Look at styles with simple lace bodices

Any sleeve style that does not incorporate ruffles, flounces, or large poufs

Traditional necklines such as jewel, bateau, square, or keyhole

A-line or fit and flare dresses with a tone on tone design in the fabric or light brocades

Choose accessories in light blues or greens

Wear a narrow jeweled belt on a sleeveless columnar dress with a square neckline

Flirty: *ROMANTIC, GLAMOROUS, BOLD, WHIMSICAL*

Your style can be many things, but it's usually tempered by a sense of girlish fun.

Look at dresses that have a lot of movement with soft skirts rather than highly fitted skirts and bodices

A-lines, fit and flare, draped, and Grecian styles

Use floral shaped embellishments in cadences of flowers at the hem or neckline

Use colored tulle in light shades of pink or blue if your personality is quieter

Wear a marigold yellow tulle crinoline if you have a vivacious personality

Wear a red tulle sash that meets at the middle in a large flower or bow if your personality is bolder and add a stone brooch at the center

Use ruffles and flounces at the hem or in tiers

When all is said and done

When you put your dress on, you should feel like the star of a film and the Oscar winner on the red carpet. You should be comfortable in your own skin with all eyes on you as you enter the room. Picture that vision you had for this day and stick to it. Only you know what's in your deepest heart of hearts so don't be dissuaded from that vision.

Your gown will be an extension of your innermost self, the fantasy we all want to live. It's not something you'll do every day, so live out your dream and your heart's reality with flair, passion, romance, and all the love you can muster for the girl inside you!

Cake Notes

Let your cake style be as much of a reflection of your dress as possible. The cake's embellishments should also resemble the line, color, style and ornamentation of your dress.

If you're wearing a white dress with a full skirt, with a sky blue sash and crinoline, opt for a white round tiered cake with blue lacy clusters in spun sugar to imitate tulle.

If you're gown is dip dyed at the bottom, do the same with your cake. Have your baker color only the bottom portion of each tier and fade it out at the edge.

If your gown is embellished heavily at the bottom and gradually diminishes toward the waist or bodice, embellish the cake the same way.

If you're using live flowers on your cake, always use the same flowers you're carrying and make sure the way they're arranged flows the same way your dress does.

If you're wearing a yellow tulle crinoline and carrying yellow flowers, have the yellow flowers on your cake only at the bottom.

If you're carrying a wire spray with glass starfish on the ends and your gown is a mermaid style, stencil a wave pattern in several shades of blue onto the cake and use silver and gold sugar to emulate foam. Long cascading bouquets should be reflected as a cadence of flowers from the cake's top to bottom.

Large, ornate, or unique flower heads can be recreated in detail onto the cake in both color and realistic size.

Destination

OF MY WEDDING

Knowing where the wedding is to be held will keep you focused on certain styles, trains, veils, and embellishments. A daytime wedding at the beach will eliminate long trains while a church wedding after five would eliminate minis, for example. This should be decided well before you make any appointments to see dresses so you can go in with a clear head and stay focused.

Weddings can take place anywhere, and the destination your wedding and your wedding reception will affect your wedding dress decisions. You may decide to be comfy and cozy while saying "I Do" indoors at a church, country club, justice of the peace, home wedding, or museum which allows for any style or length of gown.

You may decide to say "I do" in Las Vegas or in faraway France, Greece, or Italy. You may consider unusual locations such as a library, seam plant, or television studio.

Most indoor weddings allow for any type of dress fabric and level of formality. However some indoor locations such as a charming restored barn may have an uneven floor which could cause your skirt to snag.

If your wedding will take place outdoors dresses and veils that fall below the floor may become hard to control, may cause you to trip, and could become torn and dirty. Dresses with tightly fitted skirts, whether short or long, can inhibit your movement as you're trying to work your way over uneven pathways or grassy knolls. Wedding dresses with delicate or sheer fabrics and overlays will easily snag so if you'll be outside consider limiting lace, chiffon, tulle, net, voile, batiste, gossamer, organdie, satin, charmeuse, fragile embellishments, beads, or crystals to the top of your dress.

Learn about what is going to be under your feet such as walking on grass, hardwood, bricks, sand, etc. Also learn about other items that may be particular to your wedding location.

In an outdoor garden setting the weather may turn bad, the sprinkler system may turn on at any minute, or a horticulturist may have just laid down some new fertilizer. If the "floor" could cause unwanted issues with your wedding dress, consider a shorter than floor length skirt.

If your wedding will take place in an outdoor location, you will also need to consider the temperature during the time of your wedding. An outdoor winter wedding in Denver Colorado will require different fabric choices than an outdoor winter wedding in Hawaii. See the chapter on "Seasons".

With a destination wedding, at the very least, you should know if it's indoors or outdoors, at the beach, an Indian ceremonial site, the fountains at Tivoli, or the pyramids in Yucatan. Do as much research about the location as possible. You may need to do some uncomfortable traveling and you'll most likely change into your dress when you get there.

Good choices for destination wedding dresses are a sheath or Grecian style. These make a stunning classic presentation for most formalities. In this case ensure your dress is made from a blend of synthetic materials or wrinkle resistant bridal satin. Two-piece bridal suits in Dupioni silk or brocade are great for traveling. The separate top and bottom pack more easily, and the bottom can be a full style without the need for heavy under-layers or bustling. A-lines won't need the aid of a crinoline, so you can have a fuller look without a lot of fabric.

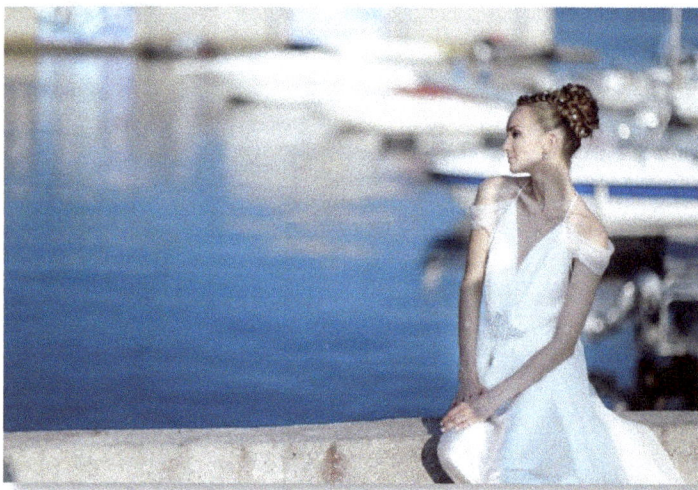

NOTE: If you're flying, you can ask to hang your dress in a closet, but carrying it around can be cumbersome. Opt for a wrinkle resistant fabric that packs well and doesn't take up a lot of space. Less fabric and weight is better than more; less layers, tiers, length, crinolines, beads, and so on.

Be aware that where you say "I Do" may also affect the pictures of you in your gown. If you choose a Japanese teahouse, they may not have room for your party or they may not allow photographs. An amusement park might cause your wedding pictures to be filled with the general public, or some overfed child may spit up on your dress. Hey- it can happen.

Event Type

HOW FORMAL IS MY WEDDING?

How formal you want your wedding event will have an effect on your choice of wedding gown and accessories. Attending a wedding is a unique experience in terms of how one should dress. The language of wedding formality is specific and if having a formal wedding you should state that on your wedding invitations.

Generally, it's better to be underdressed than overdressed but at weddings, err on the side of overdressing.

The **Formal** wedding categories are:

BLACK TIE, WHITE TIE, BLACK TIE OPTIONAL

The Basic Rules:

BRIDES: Cathedral veils should only be worn with a chapel or cathedral length gown. **Opera length gloves** (full length) are strictly formal and should not be worn at semi-formal or informal weddings. Tea length or longer dresses and elbow length or longer veils for brides are acceptable at all levels.

GROOMS: Waistcoats or vests are acceptable at all levels of formality. **Jeweled studs** or cufflinks are too dressy for daytime. They should be reserved for evening weddings with pearl studs and cufflinks worn for daytime. Tuxedos, tailcoats, and morning coats and **Cummerbunds** are considered strictly formal.

GUESTS: For men, a dark suit is always appropriate. For women, any hem that falls between the knee and the ankle or floor is generally appropriate. Any dress that falls more than 2" below floor length is inappropriate for a guest with the exception of Black Tie events.

Specific Rules:

Black Tie

A *BLACK TIE* event is considered to be the most formal of all events. The level of formality should be specifically indicated on the invitations to save guests the embarrassment of being underdressed. Black tie events take place after 5pm so if you want your wedding to be black tie and you're planning a daytime or breakfast wedding, you'll have to change your plans to evening or forgo black tie.

Brides and bridesmaids will wear full length gowns that expose no more than the tip of the foot. Cathedral veils are appropriate; however, veils can be of any length below the elbow. Hats, birdcages, sidepieces, bubbles, poufs, back pieces, clips, combs, and anything that is not a full veil is not accepted as formal enough to be considered black tie. Opera length (full length) gloves that rise above the elbow are appropriate but gloves in general are not necessary.

Female guests are expected to wear dresses which length falls to the ankle or longer.

Grooms and groomsmen will wear tailcoats, black or gray in winter, black, gray, or white in summer. The shirt should be white with studs and with French cuffs, a wing-tip collar worn with a bow tie and cuff links, cummerbund or waistcoat (vest), polished leather shoes, with or without spats.

Male guests are expected to wear tuxedos.

White Tie

WHITE TIE weddings can take place before or after 5pm and are often a choice for breakfast weddings.

For *DAYTIME,* **brides and bridesmaids** will wear dresses that fall below the knee but above the floor and from the floor and longer for *EVENING OR NIGHTTIME.*

Female guests can wear dresses of any length from knee to ankle for daytime and anywhere below the knee to floor length for evening.

For *DAYTIME, grooms* will wear morning coats with matching waistcoat and trousers, a white shirt with a pointed collar, pearl studs, and a white or gray long tie. French cuffs and pearl cufflinks are the expected style. For *EVENING,* wear tails, pearled or jeweled studs and cufflinks, a white shirt with a wing-tip collar and white bowtie, polished shoes with or without spats.

Male guests are expected to wear suits or morning coats with matching trousers for daytime and tuxedos for evening.

Black Tie Optional, Black Tie Invited, Formal

Same rules apply for the bride's and groom's attire with just a few exceptions.

The **groom** may wear a tailless coat (tuxedo) instead of a tailcoat and he may opt for a long tie instead of a bowtie.

The **bride** will still wear a formal length or longer gown and full veil.

Bowties and tuxedos are not mandatory for male guests but female guests should still feel obliged to wear ankle length or longer dresses,

Creative Black Tie

Here, you and your groom will likely be dressed formally but with a twist of some kind, such as a birdcage headpiece. The guests have the option to wear colored shirts with tuxedos or suits or more flamboyant dresses.

Semi-Formal

Brides can wear dresses of any length between the knee and the floor but full veils are still expected. Full length gloves are inappropriate as are cathedral trains and veils.

Grooms should wear a dark suit, a white shirt with a pointed collar and either French or button cuffs, and polished shoes. A waistcoat or vest is acceptable but a cummerbund is considered formal.

Male guests should wear suits in a dark color with a white shirt, or dark trousers with a white shirt and sport coat or pullover sweater, and dress shoes.

Female guests may wear dresses of any length above the floor.

Informal

INFORMAL weddings are often very casual, even to the extreme. Beach and many other outdoor weddings will fall into this category, but not all outdoor weddings are informal. As the bride, your wedding formality is dictated by the style of dress you chooses and vice versa. Formality style should be consistent.

Brides can wear dresses of any length above the floor, short gloves, and any type of head piece. Generally, veils that fall below the elbow are in the more formal range, so opt for a shorter veil.

Grooms can wear a dark suit, a light suit if the environment calls for it, or a sport coat and dark trousers. If the wedding is to be informal in the extreme, any type of attire is acceptable.

It's important for **guests** to check with the host or hostess before deciding what to wear to an informal wedding. The levels of dress vary so much that you might find yourself wearing a cocktail dress when everyone else is wearing shorts

Festive Attire

This is the least obligatory type of wedding attire. If your invitation designates that the wedding attire is to be *FESTIVE,* it's understood that you are granting guests carte blanch in choosing their outfits. You want them to be gaily dressed without restriction. Note: if you are having a theme wedding you should address that in your invitation.

Festive attire can be worn at beach weddings but also at cocktail weddings so it's important to let your guests know how **you and your groom** are planning to dress.

Please note: Dressing improperly may cause embarrassment and hurt feelings so if you are having any type of a formal or themed wedding be clear on your invitations. Your guests play an important role in making your wedding a successful and enjoyable experience and they want to be properly attired as well.

Season

OF MY WEDDING

Knowing the season and the time of day will be critical to choosing the proper fabric of your wedding dress. Once you know this, you can effectively eliminate fifty percent of the dresses out there. They won't be suitable for any number of reasons.

For example, some fabrics are only suitable for certain times of the year. Velvets and heavy brocades are cold weather fabrics while linen and organdy should be reserved for warm weather dresses. However, if you are having a destination wedding, take into consideration the possible seasonal change. If in the winter, for example, you are going to say "I do" on a beach in Hawaii that will affect your wedding dress fabric choice.

If you happen to find a dress you love but it has long sleeves and you wanted cap sleeves, this is an easy alteration. Fabrics, on the other hand, are probably not going to be something you can change in a dress.

FOR COLD WEATHER WEDDINGS CONSIDER:

Heavy fabrics such as Bengaline, Brocade, Damask, Duchesse Satin, heavier Matelassé, heavier ribbed Moiré, Panné, Peau de Cygne, Peau de Gant, Peau, de Soie, Satin Royal, stout Taffeta, and Velvet.

Substantial trims like Alencon, Battenberg, Beading, Brussels, Cordonnet, Guipure, and Soutache.

FOR WARM WEATHER WEDDINGS ASK TO SEE:

Lightweight fabrics such as Charmeuse, Chiffon, lightweight Crepes like Crepe de Chine and Crepe Georgette, Dotted Swiss, Gazar, Gossamer, Mousseline, Organdie, Organza, Tulle or Illusion, and Voile.

Light airy trims such as Chantilly, Venetian, and Ventaglio.

FOR THE INTERIM SEASONS OF SPRING AND EARLY FALL LOOK AT:

Medium weight fabrics such as Bengaline, heavier Crepe, Dupioni, Faille, Gazar, lighter weight Matelassé, Moiré, Organza, Pongee, Satin Royal, Shantung, Taffeta, Velvet Alencon, and Venise.

Almost any lace or trim as long as the fabric will support it.

Every fabric has its own unique properties. Learn more about wedding fabrics in *Fabrics for my Wedding Dress.

Your dress, headpiece, and jewelry shouldn't conflict or compete for attention so think about trims and beading, etc. as well. If one is elaborate, consider toning the other down a bit.

Best Silhouettes

FOR MY WEDDING DRESS

The *SILHOUETTE* of a dress refers to its outline or profile; the overall shape. This is the dress's most basic feature. It will set the tone and define your figure, giving it the illusion of a perfectly balanced form.

There are twelve basic silhouettes with variations:

A-line silhouette

The *A-LINE SILHOUETTE* is narrow through the waist and begins to widen in a smooth straight line at the high hip (hipbone), without gathers or curves. There is no waist seam. You may see dresses being referred to as A-line that have more fullness at the bottom causing the hemline to create waves or rippling (this is a fit and flare), but when held upright, a true A-line will end in a smooth circle at the hem.

Look closely at the waist of the dress and imagine lines extending outward, down the side of the dress to the hemline. Can you notice a triangular shape? You should! A-line gowns are the most universally flattering wedding gowns around. Why so figure friendly? They boast a slight fit in the upper portion of the body and flare gently and elegantly throughout the hips and legs. It camouflages larger hips and enhances smaller hips. They emphasize curves subtly and never cling; exposing unwanted and unsightly lumps and bumps. It slims at the waist and lengthens visually. If you have a smaller bust, opt for a detail on the bodice that adds fullness, such as draping, ruching, or an empire seam. A-lines also work well on curvy, full figures.

Ball Gown

The *BALL GOWN SILHOUETTE* is very full, round shape, like a circle. This is accomplished by the use of gathers at the waist seam and supported by a built in or separate stiff crinoline or bouffant slip of layered tulle. The skirt flows into a poufy, rounded hemline under the waist and around the hips. Crossover terms like *princess* or *full* are sometimes used to describe this silhouette. The ball dress may have a defined waist seam or princess seaming style waist without seams. The skirt will always be very full and is sometimes seen bustled or pulled up at strategic points around the skirt to create more fullness.

Most girls can carry this shape. Ball gowns help fill out a slim figure as well as highlight a defined middle. If you're very petite, keep the bodice of your dress simple so your body is not overwhelmed by cloth. Very slim girls should consider having a waist seam at the natural waist rather than dropped, with bodice details that will balance the skirt. If you're both petite and very slim, incorporate a short sleeve with some fullness, such as a petal sleeve, and a wide neckline. A hi-lo version of the ball dress will eliminate some visual weight. If you have a full waist, have the waist seam lowered an inch or two.

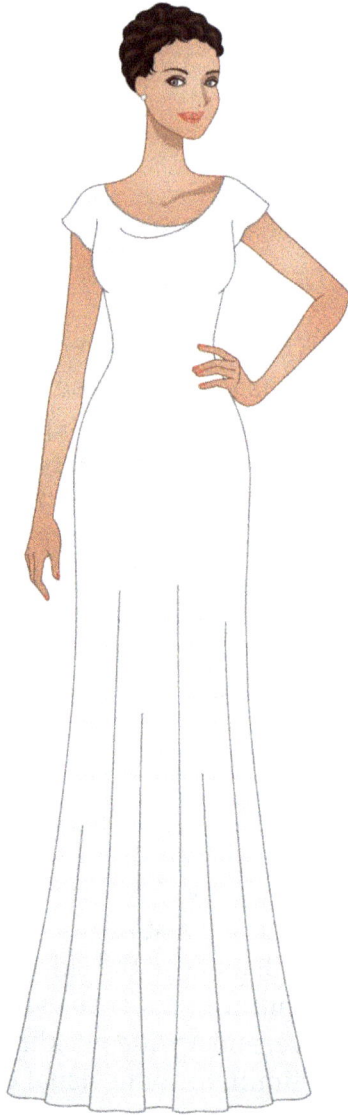

Bias

Though not actually a silhouette itself, *BIAS CUT* dresses are seen with a variety of hemline widths and can have straight, diagonal, asymmetrical or dropped waistlines, allowing the skirt to fall gracefully over the hips. Bodices can also be cut on the bias, a design common to vintage, retro, or contemporary style dresses.

The term bias is used to describe the way fabric is cut. Bias cuts are made diagonally through the grain of a length of cloth. This allows the fabric to drape fluidly over the body because the cross weave structure has been broken. It's generally not used for dresses that need to hold their shape or fullness.

Any area of your bias cut dress that is close to the body will show every detail of your undergarments, so be sure these items have no visible seaming.

Bubble

The *BUBBLE SILHOUETTE* is created by tapering the gathered skirt up and under at the hemline so that it takes on the shape of a ball, though this is not considered a ball silhouette. The ball gown is long and formal. The bubble is shorter, usually mid-thigh to knee length, and is considered informal.

Empire

EMPIRE SILHOUETTE waist gowns boast that Grecian goddess look and feel. The skirt of the empire dress is joined to the bodice by a seam placed about 1"-2" inches below the bottom of the bust. Usually this silhouette is fitted slightly below the bust and has ample draping and loose, flowing fabric that lies gently over the tummy, hips, and legs-perfect to mask larger hips. They can be fitted through the waist. You can find dresses with a decorative band at the seam join, or seams with an inverted Basque shape. A dress with a *raised waist* has its seam at the bottom of the rib cage but is often referred to as an empire waist.

This silhouette is a great option for expectant brides or any girl who is not comfortable showing her natural belly or waistline. It can have a period look when combined with a Juliet sleeve or made to be more contemporary with a portrait or off shoulder collar. The empire silhouette will always make you look longer and can accentuate the bust, especially if the bodice is gathered. This dress shape is great for lengthening a torso and giving an elongated look to shorter ladies.

Rosanna Haller

Fit and Flare

The *FIT AND FLARE SILHOUETTE* is similar to the A-line up to the point where it begins to flare. This shape is cut with a wider outward curve at the hip where the flare begins. When the fabric falls over the body, soft folds are created ending in a fuller hemline than the A-line, which has a straight smooth cut at the hip.

This silhouette is very flattering to all figure types. It's seen in every length and with a variety of necklines.

Maternity

The shape of an *EXPECTANT BRIDE* may limit some dress options, but the same rules of balance apply here as with any other figure. An empire dress will allow you a lot of freedom around the waist. If you're comfortable showing your baby bump, you can have a dress altered or made in any shape you choose.

A sheath or column dress can be dramatic; add a trumpet flare at the bottom or go strapless. Let your shoulders give you visual balance at the top. If your breasts are very full, try adding a sheer little shoulder shrug or simple 1"-2" inch straps. These straps can be wider at the base to cover more of your chest or you can opt for a sheer sleeveless inset.

Mermaid

The *MERMAID SILHOUETTE* mimics the shape of a mermaid; fitted throughout the body and made to flare dramatically beginning anywhere from the mid-thigh to the lower leg and then out to the hem by the addition of a tightly gathered long ruffle. The *trumpet* shape differs in that it's straight throughout, not always figure hugging, and flares sharply at the hem only, without the use of gathers or additions. The *fishtail* is sometimes considered a mermaid variation but the fishtail can be slim at the front. Any fullness is at the back of the dress and often there is no gathering, just insets which creates a small train or fishtail.

Your upper body shape will determine your suitability for this silhouette. Strapless bodices or puff sleeves will give some weight to the top but keep it simple. The mermaid ruffle is a powerful statement on its own. If you have an hourglass figure, no other dress will show off your curves like a mermaid silhouette.

Princess

The ***PRINCESS SILHOUETTE*** is a hybrid of the full skirt and the fit and flare. It's slim through the waist and bodice and has a very full skirt. This shape can be any length and is characterized by its fullness without a waist seam. The princess is flattering to most figure types.

Sheath or Column

The **SHEATH SILHOUETTE**, also called the column, is a straight design that does not hug the waist like the mermaid, but gently grazes the figure. Sheaths are often seen with dramatically draped necklines, wide portrait collars, keyholes, band or halter necklines, and empire waists. The defining characteristic of the sheath or column is that it drapes gently over rather than hugs the figure. Columns can have soft skirts in a Grecian style or straight structured skirts, with or without a waist seam.

This silhouette is suitable for any well-proportioned girl. But they do not provide much shaping or concealment for full figures. So if you love this shape and your waist is large, consider wearing a shorter version with a tiny pleated ruffle at the hem, a skinny belt detail, and a strapless bodice. If your hips are larger, try a column dress with a wide collar or off shoulder detail.

Tiered

The *TIERED SILHOUETTE* is a variation of a basic silhouette. Columns, A-lines, full-skirted, or empire waist dresses can all have tiers added to them, either straight around or diagonally set anywhere along the dress. They can add width and fullness to a very slim figure and when placed diagonally, can have an elongating and slimming effect.

Two Piece Suit

The *TWO PIECE SILHOUETTE* is designed like a suit, with a straight structured skirt and fitted top. Skirts for this style are usually found in knee length, ankle length, and floor length with a back or side slit. The most common top variations are either corseted or darted shells, either sleeveless with a jewel or bateau neckline or with 1/4, 1/2, or 3/4 length straight sleeves.

The suit dress is considered conservative. It's often chosen by older brides or second wedding brides. With a knee length skirt, the suit is a good choice for after-reception traveling.

When shopping for your dress, try to bring proper foundation garments so you'll get a better idea of how your preferred shapes will look on you. If you're unsure about what to bring or don't want to purchase the wrong foundation garments, talk to your consultant. She may have items in the showroom for you to use while you're trying on dresses.

Best Necklines

FOR MY WEDDING DRESS

One of the most important features in your dress is the neckline. It serves to change the dress' shape and it can really accentuate your body type. In addition to that, the *NECKLINE* is also the part of the dress that draws the most attention to your beautiful face! It should complement your facial shape, neck, shoulders, collarbone, and hair.

If your face is narrow or long, or you have a thin neck, choose a neckline with horizontal lines. If you're shoulders are wide or you're full figured, try on dresses with vertical lines. There are several neckline cuts, some with variations.

Here you will find a short guide to the most commonly chosen wedding gown necklines which include the V-neck, the sweetheart neck, the square neck, the boat neck (also known as the slot neck), the scoop neck, the surplice, the jewel, and more.

Strapless

The **STRAPLESS** bodice is usually cut straight across the front, but it can also peak on the sides or have a slight dip in the center similar to a sweetheart. Some high end designers have created variations using surplice, cowls, draping or ruching, deep center slits or Vs, and high rolled flaps similar to a man's wing tip shirt collar. If you have broad shoulders, this is good style for you. If you have a very small bust, you may be uncomfortable with this neckline unless it is perfectly fitted, which can be achieved with custom made dresses or custom alteration, or has had spaghetti straps added for a bit more security.

Asymmetrical

The **ASYMMETRICAL** neckline has two different sides. It can be a one shoulder design or, if there are two shoulders, the neckline will be cut deeper on one side, such as a square with a diagonal bottom line rather than a straight line. If you have great collar bones or a round face, this is a good style for you.

Square Neckline

The **SQUARE NECKLINE** literally forms a square around the collarbone. It can be cut closer together, creating a narrower rectangle or slot, giving it a more vertical line. This cut is complimentary to most face shapes but if you are exceptionally broad in the face, neck or shoulders, consider the narrower cut. This style is the best for those who have a large or medium bus

Sweetheart Neckline

The **SWEETHEART** neckline simply curves over the breasts and forms a heart shape around the bust line. This style can be used with or without sleeves and can have the added detail of a sheer overlay that rises, usually to the neck, and gives more visual length. It works well for those who are well endowed as it accentuates cleavage.

Scalloped Neckline

A variation of the sweetheart is the *SCALLOPED* neckline. This dress will have more than two curves, usually extending around the opening and up to the shoulders. Scallops are sometimes seen with halter neck dresses, or are cut wider across the top of the bust and narrower toward the shoulders, especially in dresses with straight fitted sleeves. Consider leaving out too many other embellishments as this neckline is both dramatic and simple. Both the sweetheart and the scallop will compliment most face shapes.

Bateau Neckline

The **BATEAU**, neckline sometimes referred to as the **BOAT** neck or **SABRINA** (think Audrey Hepburn), is a very wide oval that comes to a point as it meets the back neckline at the shoulder seam. It should follow the curve of the collar bone and can be as wide as the tips of the shoulders or extend only to the inside of the bra strap. Bateau necklines are often seen with a center front slit for interest, usually about 1-3" deep. A bateau will work well for you if you have a slender neck and face, or a small frame and is most suitable for those with a smaller bust size. If you have very wide shoulders, consider this neckline in a sleeveless dress to cut the visual width a bit.

Portrait Neckline

The **PORTRAIT** neckline, also referred to as the **PORTRAIT COLLAR,** is a wide neckline style that frames the collarbone. It's usually cut in a wide soft oval from shoulder to shoulder but can be deeper at the center or narrower across the chest. The characteristic feature of the portrait neckline is the actual collar. This is a good cut for most figure types. If you love this style but your shoulders are much wider than your hips, consider a narrower and deeper center front to draw the eye up instead of out.

Off Shoulder Neckline

The **OFF SHOULDER** neckline sits below the shoulder cap and utilizes straps that double as sleeves to give the appearance of a sleeve that has fallen off the shoulder. This is a good style for anyone with a balanced hip-to-shoulder ratio. If your shoulders are much wider than your hips, consider another style. If your shoulders are narrow and you want them to appear wider, this is a good option for you. A very wide and dramatic portrait type collar can be added in lieu of sleeves.

Jewel Neckline

The *JEWEL* neckline is a simple circle cut that follows the contours of the neck and sits at the base of the throat. Is a fantastic style if you are looking to enhance your chest. If you have a broad neck, consider an elongated front neckline instead; but if your neck is small or slim, this neckline will work well for you.

Scoop Neckline

The **SCOOP** is deeply U-shaped and usually ends no lower than about 6" below the collar bone. Also referred to as the **BALLERINA** neckline, the back of the dress is often scooped as well for a dramatic look. This style suits most types. If your face is particularly wide or angular, this shape will balance you nicely but if your face or neck is very long, consider another style, as this will make you appear longer.

V-neck Neckline

The *V-NECK* can be wide or narrow across the shoulders and ends in a point at the center front, usually anywhere from 4"- 7" inches below the collar bone. But this neckline can vary in depth depending upon the style you want. You can go with something plunging or more demure in nature. The V-neck is one of the most popular choices for wedding dresses. This style will add visual length and works especially well if you're short, or have a short neck. V-necks flatter most types. If you love this style and have a long neck or face, you don't want to add length so consider a wider V that only drops about 3" inches from the collar bone. This would be closer to a V-shaped bateau.

Surplice Neckline

A **SURPLICE** neckline is a faux wrap and a variation of the V-Neck style. Its diagonally cut symmetrical halves are crossed at the center front to form a V-shape. All the characteristics of the V-neck apply to the surplice neckline. The volume created by the overlapping pieces will enhance a smaller bust.

Keyhole Neckline

The **KEYHOLE** is a detail created by cutting a circle, oval or slit at the center top of the bodice. It can be at the front of your dress or at the back. It can be open at the top, secured with a button and loop or hook and loop closure or it can have no top opening at all. Keyholes and be discreet, that show just little skin in between the breasts or at the back, or can be more revealing. You'll find keyholes on simple necklines with plain fronts.

Queen Anne Neckline

The **QUEEN ANNE** neckline is raised at the sides and back, like a stand collar. It's a separate collar sewn onto the neck. The front neckline is almost always open and can vary into a V-shape, diamond, scoop, or sweetheart. The collar can be any height from a simple band of one inch (also referred to as a band collar) to an elaborate stand of 6-7" or more. Higher collars might roll slightly outward at the top end and the front side might have variations such as straight, rolled, pointed or wing-tipped edges. The Queen Anne neckline can be dramatic or demure and its front neckline shape will determine its suitability to various face shapes.

Halter Neckline

The *HALTER* features straps that wrap around the neck or utilizes a band around the neck to which the bodice and back are attached. The tie halter is always a backless style.

Variations of the halter dress include widely cutout sweetheart, diamond, or scoop fronts. Often, a net or lace inset is placed into the cutout. If your neck is exceptionally large, consider another style as the band or halter will add visual width to the neck.

Band and Halter Neckline

The **BAND AND HALTER** collar has an arm opening which begins at the band to bare the entire shoulder line. The back can be the same as the front or backless. Band halters often have a slit or keyhole front and the bodice is simple. The Mandarin style band does not meet completely at the front.

As with the rest of your dress, you want something that accentuates your best features and balances your shape. The neckline literally frames your face so it may be the singular most important feature in your dress.

Sleeve Length

FOR MY WEDDING DRESS

When we think of wedding dresses the first things that come to mind are the bodice and the skirt, but what about the sleeves? *SLEEVES* are just as important as the rest of the dress, if not more important. The sleeves can set the tone for the entire dress.

Choose the length of your sleeve and then the style. Many sleeve shapes can be cut to different lengths and may have different descriptive names.

If your arms are very long, opt for something that will visually cut the length. Short armed girls might try going for a long sleeve but if you're very petite, don't go past your wrist in length or your arms will look disproportionately long.

If you like a sleeve that typically covers part of hand, have the entire end portion (ruffle or addition) pulled up from the seam that joins it to the rest of the sleeve. You'll still have the look you want without the overwhelming amount of fabric.

The sleeve is the portion of your dress that extends from the top of the shoulder to any point along the arm. Sleeves can have a romantic, vintage, contemporary or architectural feel and can define the dress's mood. They can help disguise or hide any issues you may have with your arms. They can help keep you warm or cool, and their length may be dictated by the religious nature of your ceremony.

Strapless

A *STRAPLESS* (No Straps or Sleeves) dress has neither sleeves nor straps. If you need coverage for a religious venue, try adding a **coat** or **jacket** to your ensemble. This will cover part or all of your arms and can easily be removed at any time. They can be made to suit any dress, so if you have a strapless dress with a large bustle, for example, find a cropped jacket or shrug design to cover your shoulders.

Sleeveless

SLEEVELESS (Straps, no Sleeves) dresses have straps but do not have sleeves. The straps can be wide to very wide or they can be created narrow to very narrow (see Spaghetti strap). A sleeveless garment has the advantage of the unbroken line. Even if your upper arms aren't tan or toned, they will generally look longer and leaner in a sleeveless top. If your arms are beautiful, you'll rock this style.

Short Sleeve

A *SHORT* sleeve will fall from the shoulder to about 3"-4" inches down the arm. Short sleeves bisect the arm where it's widest; they can actually make arms appear larger. If you have thin upper arms, this would be a good look for you. If your arms are very long, this sleeve will visually cut the length.

Quarter Length Sleeve

1/4 length sleeves extend from the shoulder to the middle of the upper arm. Short sleeves often bisect the arm where it's widest and can actually make arms appear larger. If you have thin upper arms, this would be a good look for you. If you have larger upper arms, a ¾ length sleeve or sleeves would be a better choice.

Half Sleeve

A *HALF* sleeve falls just about to the elbow and can fall slightly above or below it. Be certain this sleeve length is not uncomfortable when you bend your arm.

3/4 Length Sleeves

3/4 length sleeves fall from the shoulder to midway between the elbow and the wrist. If you are self-conscious about your upper arms a three-quarter sleeve will both flatter and conceal.

Long Sleeves

LONG sleeves fall from the shoulder to the wrist or longer. A long-sleeve dress exudes elegance and style unlike any other style of dress. Think Princesses Kate, Diana, and Grace. For a more youthful or sexy look consider a dress with sheer or lace sleeves. When accessorizing a long-sleeved dress, take the "less is more" approach from your bracelets and earrings to shoes and hairstyles. Sheer sleeves give a dress a more modern and updated style. NOTE: If you're petite, don't go past your wrist in length or your arms will look disproportionately long.

Sleeve Types

FOR MY WEDDING DRESS

When shopping for a wedding dress you should know the most common types of *SLEEVES* so that you can make a knowledgeable choice about the overall style you are going for. Some of the most popular sleeve styles include poet, butterfly, bishop, tulip, Juliet, puff and bell.

If these words sound foreign to you, don't worry; you are not alone! Many women who have never shopped for a wedding dress have never heard of these terms.

You can be creative with your sleeves by having them made in a fabric that's different from the rest of your dress or you can opt to have one fabric element of your dress, such as tulle, lace, or illusion netting, incorporated into the sleeve.

Choose a Sleeve Style

When shopping for your perfect wedding dress, take all your sleeve options into consideration. The sleeves of your dress should match your body type, the theme of the wedding, and most of all your overall style and personality.

Angel Sleeve

ANGEL SLEEVES are a created from a square that is set into the armhole opening. They're wide and hang loosely from the shoulder. They're often seen with the outer or inner side seam left open and are found on contemporary or modern retro-styled dresses. They differ from a handkerchief sleeve (also cut in a square) in that the bottom edge is straight. A handkerchief square is turned so that the points of the square face downward toward.

Bell Sleeve

The **BELL SLEEVE** is narrow at the armhole and begins to widen from the elbow, ending in the shape of a bell at the wrist. The bell shape can be large or small but it widens evenly, without curves.

Bishop Sleeve

This ***BISHOP SLEEVE*** is long and falls naturally or is slightly gathered from the armhole, billows lightly from the elbow to the wrist area where it is gathered into a pretty puff at the cuff. The bishop sleeve is one that takes one back to yesteryear. The design is something you would expect to see in a period film where all the men and women dressed to impress. Think along the lines of the sleeves on the dresses that women wore in the French Quarter or in the days of the civil war and you will have an image of the bishop sleeve.

Butterfly Sleeves

Similar to a bell sleeve in shape, but generally not longer than 4-5 inches, the *BUTTERFLY SLEEVE* usually does not go completely around the arm. The butterfly sleeve is one that gives you the feeling of wearing wings on your arms. This style brings in the romance of the poet sleeve with a touch of innocence..

Cap Sleeve

The **CAP SLEEVE** is very small and covers only the top of the shoulder (*shoulder cap*). This sleeve is not really attached at all but is part of a strap. It does not cover the underarm; instead, the under edges taper gracefully back into the armhole leaving the underarm exposed. If you have slender and beautiful arms, it is the sleeve to show them off.

Capelet Sleeves

The **CAPELET SLEEVE** falls several inches below the elbow in a soft flare resembling a cape; similar to a wide bell.

Dolman Sleeves

The **DOLMAN SLEEVE** is cut in one piece with the bodice of the dress. There is no shoulder seam. The armscye (armhole) is long and can extend to the waist. This sleeve is very wide throughout ending in a fitted wrist cuff that can be anywhere from one inch to as much as 6-7 inches wide.

Fitted Sleeve

A *FITTED SLEEVE* can be any length and will fit snuggly the entire length of the sleeve, from shoulder seam to hem.

Gauntlet Sleeves

A *GAUNTLET* is a separate cuff usually not higher than the elbow; similar to a glove but without finger coverings, it has a loop at the lower edge allowing it to be held in place by slipping over the middle finger.

Gibson Sleeves

The **GIBSON SLEEVE**, named for the famous Gibson Girls penned by 19th century illustrator, Charles Dana Gibson, begins with a large puff at the shoulder and is fitted at the forearm; also called a leg-o-mutton or gigot sleeve because it resembles the animal's hind leg.

Gigot Sleeves

GIGOT (pronounced jig-ut) in French refers to the back leg of an animal, especially a lamb or sheep. The *gigot sleeve* is wide at the top and fitted at the bottom. Boning and padding are used to hold the shape of the large puff at the shoulder.

You'll see gigots with large puffs that extend past the elbow, billowing more at the bottom before they attach to the fitted forearm piece, or rounded puffs ending in a ruffled peplum over the tapered lower portion, or simple gigots that are all one piece, being lightly puffy at the top and tapering gradually toward the wrist.

Halter Sleeves

The **HALTER SLEEVE** is actually a neckline style. But a halter is always sleeveless. If you have beautiful shoulders, back, and arms this is a good look for you.

Handkerchief Sleeves

The *HANDKERCHIEF SLEEVE* is cut from a square or rectangle with one edge sewn into the shoulder seam. It's turned so that the pointed ends of the square are facing downward and is often seen with the under seam left open.

Juliet Sleeves

The **JULIET SLEEVE** is named for Shakespeare's famed heroine in *Romeo and Juliet*. It's gathered into the shoulder seam to create a small to medium puff that may extend to the middle of the upper arm. It's then gathered into a fitted lower sleeve. This is a long sleeve and often falls past the wrist with an added ruffle or flounce. This sleeve is not good for women with large arms as it tends to make them look broader upwards.

Poet Sleeves

The term *POET SLEEVE* is given to two types of long sleeves. The first is fitted from the shoulder to just below the elbow then flares dramatically to the wrist in a trumpet shape or has a long soft ruffle added at the elbow which falls to the hand. The second variation is lightly gathered or pleated into the shoulder seam and falls to or just above the wrist where it's again lightly gathered into a band and has a ruffle or flounce added that falls over the hand.

Puff Sleeves

The **PUFF SLEEVE** is just what it sounds like; sleeves that puff out! It's gathered into the shoulder seam, widens over the arm in a bubble, and is then gathered into a band or piped hem. The puff sleeve gives a feminine look when applied to wedding gowns. There are several ways to apply this look to your wedding dress, from short puffs to quarter length sleeve puffs. A short ruffle is sometimes added around the bottom.

Raglan Sleeves

The *RAGLAN SLEEVE* is not set into a shoulder seam. Instead, the seam join runs diagonally from the neck to the underarm with the sleeve draping over the shoulder and arm. This sleeve is more common to wedding shrugs and jackets of sheer organza or dresses created in a modern retro-style.

Set-in Sleeves

A **SET-IN SLEEVE** is any sleeve that is attached to a strap of the dress along the shoulder line. Set-in is not an actual sleeve but a sewing term of how a sleeve is attached to a garment.

Spaghetti Straps

SPAGHETTI STRAPS are very thin, and look like pieces of spaghetti, hence, their name. For brides who are uncertain about the security of a completely strapless style, this may be a good alternative.

Tulip Sleeves

The **TULIP SLEEVE**, also known as the petal sleeve, is a short sleeve cut from two or more pieces that extend from the shoulder seam and cross over each other to cover the upper arm. The tulip sleeve is one that is regarded as girly and ultra-feminine. Tulips are short, petite little sleeves that are designed with a split structure. This makes them both comfortable to wear, showing the fashion does not have to be confining.

Bodice Types

BODICE is the term applied to the portion of a dress that is above the waist or waist seam. Its shape is obtained by the use of darts and seams and often has an underlying structure of boning, facings and interfacings.

As with the rest of your dress, the bodice should be proportionate to your frame and its shape should be in balance. This is an area where you can have details added, flourishes, stones, lace, beading, or embroidery, all of which will contribute to the dress's overall mood.

Almost all wedding dress bodices fit rather closely to the body. The bodice is then customized by the shape of the neckline, sleeves, the cut of the waistline, embellishments and details. You'll rarely find a bodice that is not fitted, such as blousons or kimono styles.

Boning Style Bodice

BONING is a way to support and give a rigid shape to the dress bodice, usually by means of flexible steel wires (i.e.: "bones.") Advantages of a boned dress include clean lines, side seams that stay straight, and a bodice that is guaranteed never to sag or appear ill-fitted. Boning is also indispensable to preserve a V-shaped waistline at the bottom of the bodice. A wedding gown with boning gives a very regal and Victorian feel, and is often seen in corsets and strapless dresses. Excessively boned dresses support and give definition to plus-size brides, but can sometimes overwhelm a more petite bride.

Corset Bodice

CORSET style bodices fit very closely to the body. Darted seams are used at the front and back princess lines to draw the fabric in and shape it. (These are the imaginary lines that run down from the shoulder line, cross over the apex of the bust, and continue down through the waist). They are then boned at the four princess seams and the two side seams, interlined and lined. Boning consists of inserting strips of stiff nylon, plastic, or horsehair into pockets that have been constructed into the interlining of the corset. They're necessary for holding your corset in place. Corsets can be laced at the front or back, or have a back or side zipper.

Crumb Catcher Bodice

A *CRUMB CATCHER* is a bodice design typically found on strapless bodices or bodices with very wide necklines. This piece is constructed from a stiff fabric with an interfacing of horsehair or some other structural netting, then draped or ruched across the front of the bodice at the neckline. It's designed to stand up and away from the dress. An inner modest panel fits closely to the body behind the crumb catcher. This detail will add visual weight to the bodice and can enhance a small bust or narrow back and shoulders.

Draped Bodice

The **DRAPED** bodice has its fabric gently gathered into one side, forcing diagonal folds to occur. This will create a slimming effect.

Inset Bodice

An *INSET* or *INSERT* is a piece of fabric that is placed into the body of a dress, usually made of a sheer fabric or netting. This is a design detail and not a bodice type. The inset can be placed into a cutout, keyhole, or low neckline or can be placed directly over the dress fabric.

Keyhole Bodice

The **KEYHOLE** is a design detail consisting of a cutout at or near the center neckline. It can be small or large, slit, round or oval, and can be left open or filled with an inset.

Overlay Bodice

An *OVERLAY* is a sheer or lace fabric that is layered on top of the dress bodice to add fullness and softness simultaneously. This is great for vintage 1920s-style dresses and lends itself beautifully to wedding dresses of any style.

Ruched Bodice

RUCHED bodices are created by gathering fabric into the side seams of the basic structure, giving it a softer draped effect. The difference between the two is that ruching folds are more evenly spaced and draping folds give the appearance of being randomly placed.

Surplice Bodice

A *SURPLICE* is created by diagonally crossing two lengths of fabric. You can have a surplice effect neckline or you can have the entire front of the bodice surpliced. The effect of the diagonal folds will give the illusion of length and can make you appear slimmer, especially if the bodice falls below the natural waist, as with dropped waist or even mermaid style dresses.

The type of bodice you choose will depend mostly on three things; what type of style you really like, the time of year you are getting married (and the venue), and the shape of your figure.

Waistlines

FOR MY WEDDING DRESS

The *WAISTLINE* is the term applied to the seam that joins the bodice of a garment to its skirt. Thanks to expert pattern engineering and tailoring, dress waistlines can be placed at any point between the bottom of the bust and the low hip.

Balance is the key to determining which waistline is right for your wedding dress. Its strategic location can enhance your strong points or draw the eye away from figure flaws.

There are seven basic types of waistlines, all of which can have slight variations, especially at the back of the dress.

Asymmetrical Waistline

ASYMMETRICAL waistline seams run diagonally across the dress and can be placed beginning at the natural waist or dropped to almost any location on the skirt. This is the most creative waistline from a design viewpoint. If you are having a custom dress made, consider two asymmetrical seams that cross each other below the hip for a very sophisticated modern look. The Asymmetrical waist offers options for many body types.

Basque

BASQUE waistlines will sit near the hip bone at the sides and curve down about 5"-7" inches at the center front. The defining feature of the Basque is a U or V shape which may also be cut into the back waist. The fabric that is gathered into the waist seam will serve to camouflage and minimize overly full hips and will accentuate natural curves on most figure types.

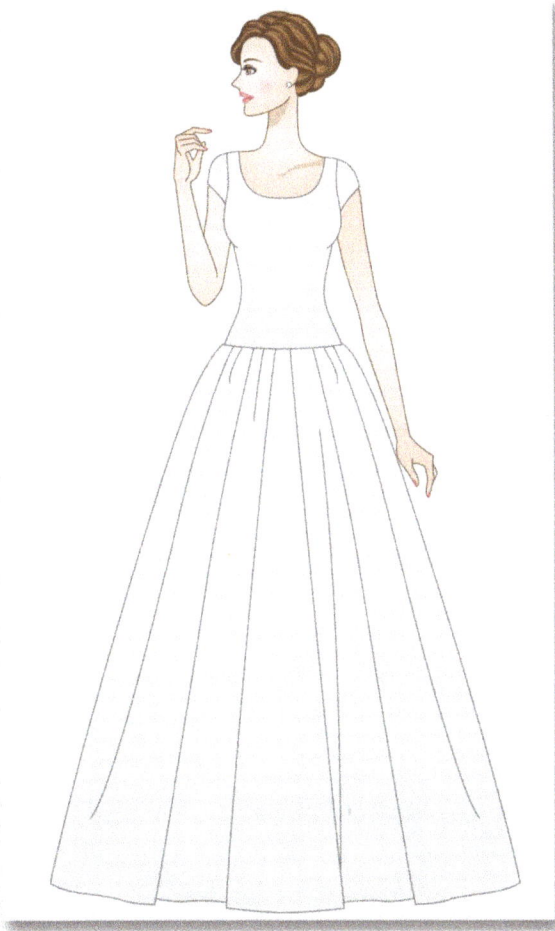

Dropped Waistline

The *DROPPED* waist can sit anywhere from 3" to 6" inches or more below the natural waist. This is usually a horizontal seam join so the result will be the illusion of a longer torso. Be sure to have your advisor assess the balance in your appearance with this waistline. You don't want your legs to appear short and the balance may depend on the neckline, the length of the dress, the train, and any overlays.

Empire Waistline

The **EMPIRE** waistline is a horizontal join or seam placed about 1" inch below the bust. If the skirt is cut with a bit of fullness, it will hide a larger waist or belly and draw the eye up, emphasizing the bust. This style works for most average figure types but consider avoiding it if your bust is disproportionately large or if you're over 5'10" inches tall.

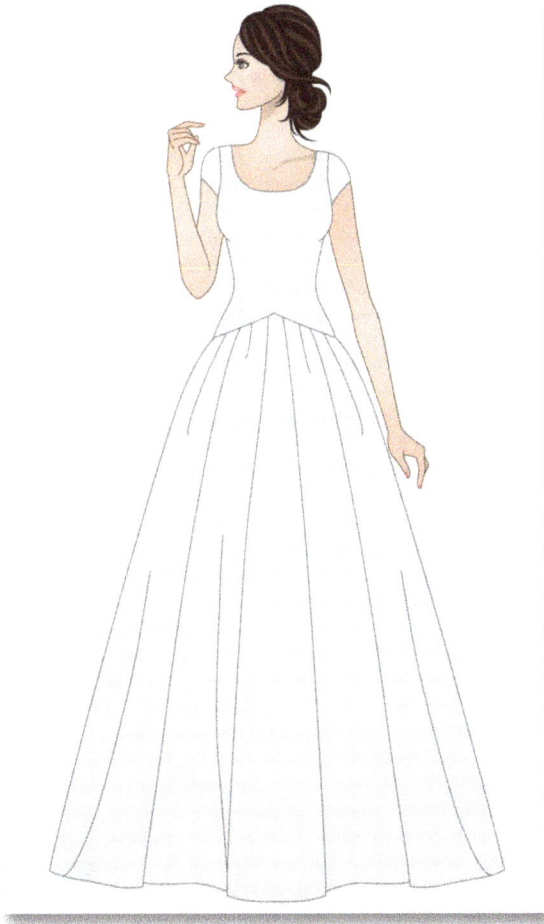

Inverted Basque Waistline

The *INVERTED BASQUE* is essentially the opposite shape of a Basque waist. It crosses the body below the natural waistline and forms an upward pointing central peak or inverted curved V-shape.

Natural Waistline

The **NATURAL** waistline is a horizontal seam located where the body's natural waistline sits, just above the navel. This waist may have a Basque style back or a straight back waistline. The horizontal front will visually cut the figure in half, so if you're tall this is a good option for you. If your waist is larger than your hips, there are other styles that will enhance your figure. For most figure types, the Natural waistline is a flattering style.

Princess Seamed

PRINCESS SEAMED (No Waist) dresses are considered a waistline style, though there is no waist seam. Princess seams are actually long separate pieces of fabric engineered into the dress pattern which are designed to draw the fabric in at the waist, following the curves of the natural waistline. Any amount of fullness can be cut into the skirt from A-line to very full depending upon how the long pieces of fabric are cut.

Skirt Lengths

FOR MY WEDDING DRESS

Wedding dress *SKIRTS* can range in *LENGTH* from scandalously short to dramatically long. A skirt's hem will be anywhere from just a few inches below the crotch to the floor and even longer, especially on formal and royal wedding dresses.

Some skirt's lengths are named for where they fall on the body
such as *mini* and *knee*, and some for the function to which they
were typically worn, such as *cocktail* and *intermission.* The
length of your dress will determine the formality of your
wedding and vice versa so if you don't want a formal wedding,
for example, don't choose a six foot train on a floor length
dress.

Traditionally, a bride and groom would change from their
wedding attire into suits before leaving directly for a
honeymoon. Many brides with a formal wedding agenda are
choosing a second dress in a shorter length, one that allows
them more freedom to play at the reception and which they
can wear on the way to their honeymoon destination.

Mini Length Skirt

The *MINI LENGTH* skirt usually falls no longer than mid-thigh and is suitable only for informal or destination weddings.

Cocktail Length Skirt

Contemporary *COCKTAIL LENGTH* dresses typically fall 2"-3" inches *above* the knee while **traditional** *COCKTAIL LENGTH* falls 7"-9" inches *below* the knee (see Intermission); contemporary cocktail length is strictly informal.

Knee Length Skirt

KNEE LENGTH falls just at the knee or slightly above or below it and is suitable for informal or destination weddings.

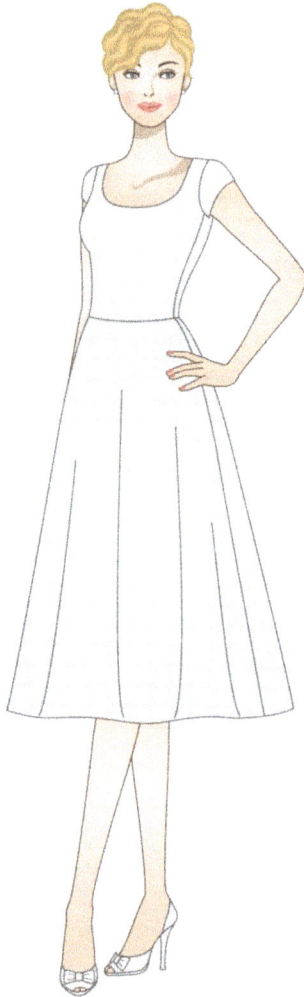

Tea/Midi Length Skirt

TEA LENGTH falls to 2"-6" inches below the knee, about to the middle of the calf or slightly longer and is suitable for semi-formal or destination weddings.

Intermission Length Skirt

Traditionally, *INTERMISSION LENGTH* falls somewhere below the bottom of the calf but higher than the top of the ankle and is suitable for semi-formal weddings. Intermission was the original cocktail length.

Hi-Lo Length Skirt

HI-LO LENGTH is typically a combination of intermission length at the front and floor length at the back. It may be seen in other lengths but the back is always longer than the front. This type of dress is suitable for informal to semi-formal weddings, depending on the length of the *front* of the dress.

Ballerina Length Skirt

The *BALLERINA LENGTH* dress has a full skirt and reaches to just above the ankle. This dress is suitable for semi-formal weddings.

Ankle Length Skirt

ANKLE LENGTH is ideally hemmed just to the middle of the ankle so part of the ankle shows but it is often seen hemmed just below the ankle. A dress is considered ankle length as long as it does not reach the top of the foot. This length is suitable for semi-formal weddings.

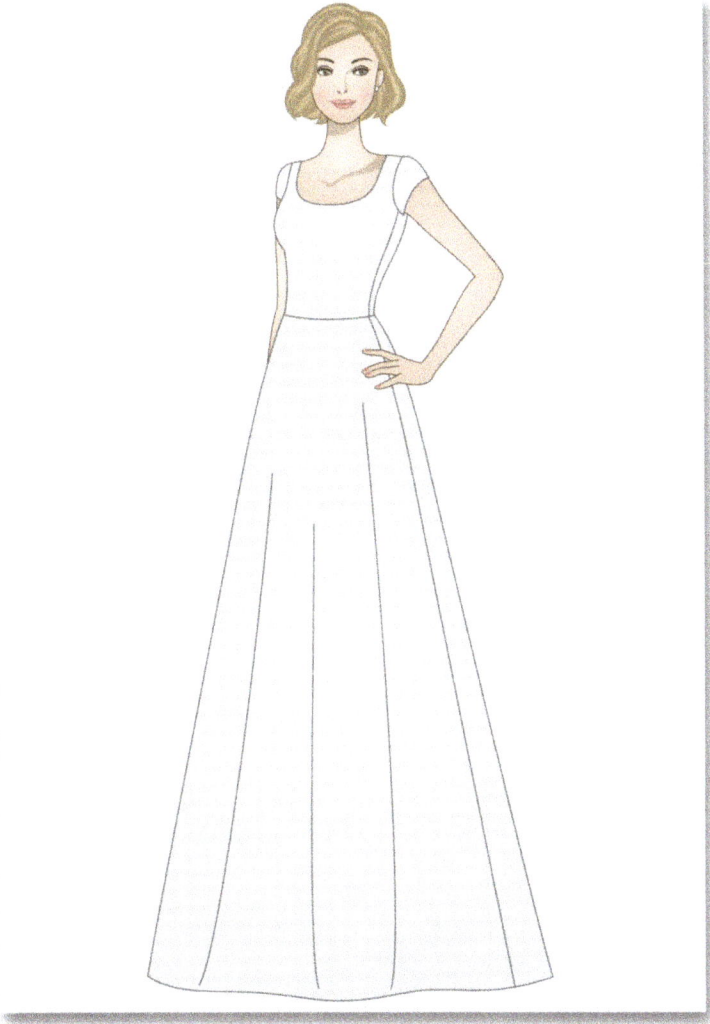

Floor Length Skirt

FLOOR LENGTH should reach to the top of the back of the heel or just barely graze the floor and is suitable for formal weddings.

Ball Length Skirt

BALL LENGTH hits the floor and reaches beyond the bottom of the heel. This is typically a full skirted dress and is suitable for formal weddings only.

After you've determined the formality or informality of your wedding and decided on your preferred dress length, keep your body type in mind. Any hemline that falls between the bottom of the knee and the ankle will cut your legs off a bit. Anything above the knee or below the ankle will lengthen your leg's appearance. A skirt's shape, whether full or slim, should be balanced at the bodice and sleeve. Remember, before trying on dresses, to find a pair of shoes with the same heel height you'll be wearing on the big day.

Skirt Types

FOR MY WEDDING DRESS

SKIRT** is the term applied to the portion of a garment that falls below the waistline seam or visual waist if there is no seam.

You'll find skirts on dresses, coats, and even men's suits. For example, the tailcoat style dinner jacket has a split skirt at the back with the front cut out, and is called a *cutaway*.

Dress skirts (with the exception of a princess line) will always be joined to the bodice at the waist seam. You'll always want to find a balance between the skirt and the bodice and much of this may depend on your body type and/or the embellishments you choose. Your advisor can assist you in determining the right balance for you within your style preferences.

There are fourteen basic types of wedding dress skirts in vogue today, some of which have variations in style.

Gathered Skirt

A *GATHERED SKIRT* is a length of fabric which has been gathered at one edge (bunching the fabric together) causing the fabric to puff out and give it volume. It is then sewn into a seam or joined to another piece by a seam. (Look at the waistline). It's often used as an embellishment to a dress or can be used on a sleeve. Ballerina style skirts are an example of a gathered skirt.

Circle Skirt

For a **CIRCLE SKIRT,** the fabric is cut in a circular shape, like a donut. The center is cut out of the circle and this inside opening is then attached to the waist line. The longer outside edges of the circle form a wavy ripple or flounce. Typically, the entire skirt will be cut this way so that the hem edge falls into a wide ripple. This is a great cut for straighter styles if you want your dress to end with a flourish. A circle skirt will add less bulk around one's waist so if you want to look thinner at the waistline, this may be a good look for you.

True Overskirt

A *TRUE OVERSKIRT* lies over the main skirt and covers the back, the sides, and part of the front, leaving the center front open so the main skirt is visible. True overskirts are most commonly designed to be about 1"-2" inches shorter than the main skirt. A regal or medieval overskirt might be several inches or more long than the main skirt and act as a train.

Petal Overskirts

PETAL OVERSKIRTS are multiples of oval or petal shaped pieces (though technically they can be any shape) that overlap each other, like flower petals, over the main skirt.

Bias Cut Overskirt

A *BIAS CUT OVERSKIRT* will lend fluidity to the second layer and help eliminate a potentially bulky appearance. Fabric that is cut on the bias or diagonal grain will fall more softly than straight-of-grain cuts. Any shape can be cut on the bias so this is not really a style as much as a technique for cutting a style. Bias cutting weakens the stability of the fabric, however, and your consultant should be able to tell you if this is inadvisable based on the fabric of your dress.

Draping Skirt Type

When excess fabric has been gathered into the back or side seam, the result is a *DRAPING* effect. This detail is engineered into the pattern before it is cut. It adds fullness and interest to the garment and works best if the dress length is long. Draping can be added anywhere along a seam.

Streamers and Tails

STREAMERS are narrow and usually fall somewhere just above, below, or right at the skirt hem on shorter skirts. They may extend to anywhere between the knee and the hem on longer skirts.

TAILS are two wide panels which fall from the waist (or less commonly the shoulders or mid-back) over the back of the skirt. Though shorter lengths are less common, they can be any length and are often seen extending beyond the hemline for dramatic effect. Tails are named after a man's tailcoat.

Accordion Pleated Skirt

ACCORDION PLEATS are folds in the fabric that resemble the
bellows of an accordion. They can be any width and the folded
edges all face in the same direction (they are laid flat in one
direction when being sewn into the waist). Accordion pleats
work for a slim figure where the pleats are allowed to fall
naturally rather than being pulled open by the shape of the
body. If, when in a straight standing position, the pleats of your
skirt pull open more than just a little, this style is not for you.

Box Pleated Skirt

BOX PLEATS are folded to resemble three sides of a box. The inverse is the same as the front so when laid flat, it appears as though there are slits in the fabric. Because box pleats expand quite a bit and may add some visual width, bridal box pleats are usually limited to two or four wide pleats across the front and/or back. This gives the illusion of flat panels with the added benefit of built in ease. If, when in a straight standing position, your pleats pull open more than just a little, this style is not for you.

Tiered Skirt

A skirt that is *TIERED* has a basic skirt with one or more skirts falling beneath it. This series of layers is not bulky because only the top tier begins at the waist with each ascending tier falling over the seam join of the tier below it. Tiers of any width can be horizontal or diagonal and the number of tiers can have a dramatic effect on the overall appearance of your dress. This style works very well with lightweight fabrics and can be very regal in heavier weights.

Bubble Style Skirt

This skirt is fitted at the waist and widens into a puff or **bubble** near the bottom where it then tucks back toward the body creating a soft blousy hemline.

Fit and Flare

The *FIT AND FLARE* skirt fits snugly through the waist and hips and then begins to widen, or flare, in beauty and elegance to swirl romantically around the feet. Because this style can disguise imperfections while enhancing every line of a woman's shape it works for nearly every body type; large, small, curvy, or straight. The skirt can be a single or layered piece, feathered, overlaid, or gathered for a dramatic to a romantic look. Sometimes it is confused with the *MERMAID* or *TRUMPET* skirts which begin their flare at or below the knee.

Trumpet Style Skirt

The *TRUMPET* is long and straight, softly flaring around the hem and is similar in shape to a trumpet flower. This cut can be achieved by engineering the pattern piece for a light flare or by adding gored insets during construction, which creates deeper folds in the trumpet, giving the shape more impact.

The *TRUMPET* and the *MERMAID* are similar in that they are both slim and tapered. Both follow the lines of the body and flare out below the knee.

Mermaid Style Skirt

The *MERMAID* is long and straight but more fitted below the knee and ends more dramatically. The look is achieved by the addition of a gathered piece that resembles the lower portion of a mermaid's body, the fin. Tighter gathers and more fabric will give a fuller bottom.

Fanback Style Skirt

The *FANBACK* is long and straight with a *pleated* inset that begins as a narrow point and widens dramatically as it reaches the floor. It's usually longer than the front hem, giving it a striking back appeal.

The *FANBACK* or *FISHTAIL* are the same except for the gore or inset at the back of the skirt, which can begin anywhere along the center back from the waist to the knee.

Fishtail Style Skirt

The **FISHTAIL** is long and straight with a flat or *non-pleated* inset. It also begins as a narrow point and widens dramatically as it reaches the floor.

Bustled Skirt

The *BUSTLE* is a style detail of a wedding dress skirt (See Types of Bustles) designed to mimic the 19th century under frame used to support the shape of heavy dresses and petticoats. The modern bridal bustle is essentially excessive fabric or an overskirt which has been pulled into an exaggerated gather at the center back of the skirt, usually at the hip line. It's common to see trains which are designed to be pulled up into a bustle and held in place by hook and loop or button and loop fasteners. The bustle will flatter most figure types.

Dress skirts vary and you'll often find elements of two styles incorporated into one skirt. For example, the bubble can be tiered for an exquisite look (see our example above under "bubble"), a true overskirt might have streamers at the front where it meets the main skirt giving it a Renaissance feel, or a simple, straight cut, knee length skirt might have a whimsical gathered tulle overskirt.

BUSTLING: When you try on a dress with a train, ask to see how it will look bustled up. Some trains can only be bustled a certain way and you may dislike the silhouette once it's up.

Length and Types of Trains

FOR MY WEDDING DRESS

The length of your dress will dictate the formality of your wedding and most *TRAINS* extend beyond the dress length.

If you want to be more formal for a church or religious wedding but not for the reception, opt for a removable train or one that can be bustled, allowing you to move freely.

Designers tend to classify their train lengths differently, so don't rely completely on the train's name. Trains are generally classified by their length with a starting point at the back waist, a marker of the floor or hemline, and how far past that marker the train extends. You can always have your train altered to suit your size and your consultant should be able to have the train pinned up for you in the showroom.

There are seven general types of wedding dress trains and train lengths are always measured from the back waist. The various types and lengths of trains listed here will help you make an informed decision as to the type you want.

BUSTLING: When you try on a dress with a train, ask to see how it will look bustled up. Some trains can only be bustled a certain way and you may dislike the silhouette once it's up.

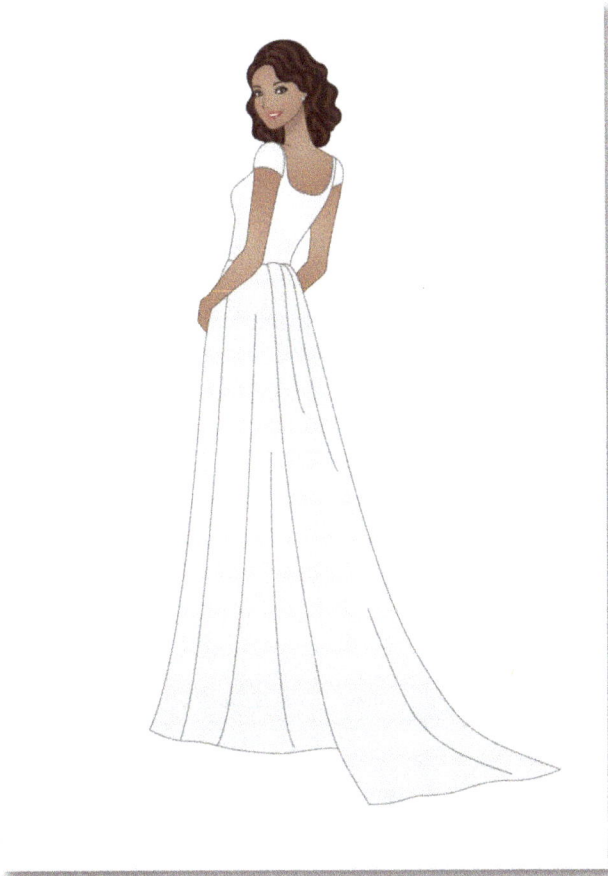

Panel Style Train

The **PANEL** train is a simple separate piece of fabric that is attached to the back of the dress at any point between the shoulders and the waist. It can be gathered or straight, or it can be attached at one point of the square, allowing the fabric to cascade in a diamond shape. Panels can end in a straight hem or oval hem and can be of any length, its defining characteristic being its flat panel configuration. They are typically detachable and for the modern bride, they offer contemporary versatility between the ceremony and the reception.

Watteau Style Train

The **WATTEAU** train attaches to the top of the dress, at or just below the shoulder seam or at the top back edge of a low back or strapless dress. It can be centered between the shoulder lengths in one panel, divided into two panels, one on each side, or a dress can have only one shoulder panel. Less commonly, Watteaus have been placed at the shoulder's front and back. Watteau trains traditionally end at the dress hem but it's becoming more common to see Watteaus of any length. Watteau panels can be made to be detachable.

Sweep Style Train

The *SWEEP* train, also referred to as the *BRUSH* train, is designed to just graze or sweep the floor as you walk. It's short but it's still a train and will trail below the hem of your dress anywhere from one to two feet. If you're looking for a dress that bustles for your reception, be sure to inform your consultant. Bustling requirements are different for every length train and this train won't make a large bustle.

Court Length Train

The **COURT** train extends approximately three feet behind the dress as measured from the natural waist. This train takes its name from the days when ladies appeared at court. It was a matter of unacceptable etiquette for a lady's train to extend beyond that of the royalty whose act of grace allowed her to be in their presence.

Chapel Length Train

The *CHAPEL* train extends to about four feet behind the dress as measured from the natural waist. The train takes its name from its suitability to smaller churches or chapels where the longer, more traditional train was inappropriate or cumbersome. Chapel trains tend to have the same fullness at the back as a longer train without the weight and are suitable for all wedding types from informal to formal.

Cathedral Length Train

CATHEDRAL trains are formal and can extend up to eight feet behind the dress. The name is derived from the vast interiors of Roman cathedrals. Depending on the fabric they can be very weighty so many times are pulled up near the center of the length and hooked to the back of the waist, essentially folding the train up or seen bustled at three points along the back of dress creating three poufs down its length. If you want the look without the weight, opt for a cathedral veil instead. It will give you the same length and drama without the weight.

Monarch Style Train

The *MONARCH* train goes by many names - *ROYAL, REGAL, ROYAL CATHEDRAL, GRAND CATHEDRAL, EXTENDED CATHEDRAL.* It requires a grand space to showcase its extensive length of nine feet or more and a fit bride to carry its weight. This train is not meant for bustling.

The monarch is rarely seen today with the exception of royal weddings which is where the style originated.

When choosing your dress, train, and veil always express your desire or intent to bustle. Dresses and trains do not come with bustling attachments in place. Various fabrics, lengths, and the bride's stature all play a part in how the train will be bustled and at which points. Your bridal consultant will be able to help you with this in the showroom by demonstrating the bustling of individual trains.

Bustle Types

FOR MY WEDDING DRESS

A simple *BUSTLE* is created by pulling the train up and over the dress and securing it to a seam. The bustle is attached at the seam because there are several thicknesses of fabric here which will better support the weight of the train. The resulting multiple folds are ideal for full gowns or long trains.

If your wedding dress has a train of any length, it will undoubtedly add to the elegance of your walk down the aisle. Trains and veils can be magnificent and graceful, but in the same way you'll want to remove a long veil for convenience and comfort during your reception, you'll want to eliminate the cumbersome train during the festivities. Dancing, mingling with guests and even sitting at the head table will all be easier if you bustle your train.

Wedding dresses do not come with bustling

If you choose any style train, your advisor will likely suggest you have bustling inputs added to your dress. If she doesn't suggest it, be sure to ask. Bustles need to be lifted to the point where the hemline runs evenly around the dress, not longer. This is why they're custom added later on, during the alteration stage.

Buttons and loops, hooks and eyes, or ribbons will be added according to the length of your train, the style and fabric of your dress, your physical stature, and the bustle style you want - *Over Bustle, French (Under) Bustle, Tufted Bustle,* or *Austrian Bustle* to name a few.

If your train is shorter than double the length from your waist to the dress hem, the bustling can be attached below the waist so that the hemlines can meet or you can be creative and bring your bustle above the hemline. Some brides will leave a 8"-10" inches of train below the floor.

Over bustles are usually secured by a button and a loop, but you can use a hook and eye instead. The button or eye will be attached to the waist seam and the loop or hook will face inward. Be sure the button and eye or hook and eye set is designed to be used on bridal gowns. They're wrapped with silk thread and they're heavy construction will not bend.

One Point Bustle

The *ONE POINT* over bustle is very inexpensive. If you choose to create your own bustle attachment, use a covered shank button on the outside secured with a flat anchor button on the inside of the dress. This will prevent the outer button from pulling at the stress point. Measure the train by having someone hold it up so that the hemlines match and mark the spot for a loop. Using color matched buttonhole twist, machine stitch a loop large enough to hang over the button.

The one point bustle is not strong enough to support heavy fabrics or long trains and it will often tear even with lighter fabrics.

Two Point Bustle

A **_TWO POINT_ over** bustle is created by securing the train evenly at the bodice seam approximately 1"-2" inches on each side of the center back seam.

Three Point Bustle

A *THREE POINT* over bustle is more secure still with a center point and two side points.

Ballroom Bustle

The most dramatic **over** bustle is the ***BALLROOM BUSTLE*** or ***DIANA BUSTLE***. This is created by spreading the train across the bodice seam join to within 2" inches of the side seams and will require 9-11 evenly spaced connections. Cathedral and regal trains, which measure up to 9' foot in length, lend themselves to this type of bustling. The result is often imperceptible and can appear to be part of the dress design.

French Bustle

The *FRENCH*, or under bustles are tucked under the dress fabric rather than pulled over it. They are created by using a series of ribbons or buttons and loops that run vertically or in a triangular shape on the underside of the dress. They are particularly suited to dresses that have most of their embellishment at the top of the skirt. If you've chosen a long train and prefer the under bustle, your bustle will have multiple luxuriant folds at the back. Under bustles can be used on trains of any length or fabric resulting in a silhouette that billows out over the bottom of the dress. Under bustles can also be made to fall anywhere on the back of the dress, regardless of the length of your train.

The Tufted Bustle

A **TUFTED BUSTLE** is used on dresses with tufts built into the design of the dress or train. A tuft is created by gathering fabric to a central point, similar to a flower, and often with a stone, pearl, or appliqué at the center. Each tuft pickup will be strategically placed so as not to distort the built-in tufted design of the dress. The effect is a cascade of draping billows or poufs reminiscent of storybook princesses.

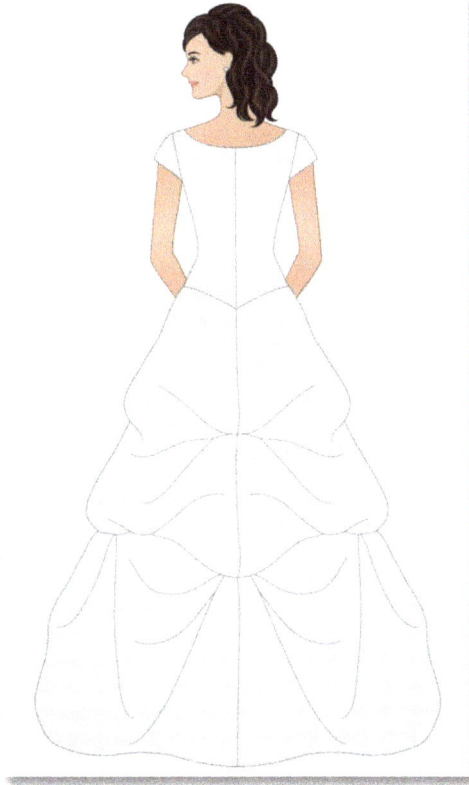

The Royal Bustle

The *ROYAL BUSTLE* is a type of tufted **under** bustle and is created by gathering up and fastening multiple pick-ups in various places resulting in small poufs or billows. It differs from the tufted bustle in that the train does not have tufts built into its design. The tuft pattern can be created in any configuration, randomly placed to fill the entire back skirt, or arranged in a vertical or triangular pattern around the center back seam of the dress. The royal bustle lends itself well to full gowns and cathedral trains and the pick-up points can be further embellished with bustle accessories. This style is particularly striking on dresses with a colored godet at the back.

The Austrian Bustle

The **AUSTRIAN BUSTLE** is created by building a casing into the underside of the dress over the center seam. A ribbon is run through the length of the casing and lightly pulled, causing the dress to pull together. This bustle is simple and works for shorter trains with lightly full skirts. If your dress is full enough, consider using three evenly spaced vertical Austrian strings for a fuller effect.

Your Unique Bustle

Some bridal dresses are designed with pickups in place around the front of the skirt. Your bustling should match the pickup design of the rest of the dress.

Bridesmaid's dresses can also be bustled. Consider allowing your bridesmaids to bustle their dresses differently than yours.

You can get even more creative by bustling the sides of a full dress or pulling your train up higher than the dress hemline and exposing part of a tulle underskirt or crinoline. If you're planning to do this, consider wearing an opaque under-slip in addition to the underskirt if modesty is a concern.

If you like the way a bustled silhouette looks when attached at the waist or any other point, even though the hemlines may not meet, certainly do that. Your bustle will be unique and appear as a flounce or peplum, a ruffle or intended embellishment. Incorporating bustle accessories such as bows, flowers, tulle clips, or a brooch will help customize your dress and add color.

NOTE: The original *BUSTLE* was not part of a garment at all. Popular during the 18th and 19th centuries in various forms, it was a rigid metal or mesh frame or padding worn under a dress and tied around the waist to support the exaggerated yards of lavish, sometimes ornate, and heavy materials used in everyday dresses.

"Bustles should be long and narrow, and consist of twelve steel springs encased in muslin and kept in place with elastic bands. It should add nothing to the breadth of the hips but is required to push the skirts out backward..." Peterson's Magazine, September 1873. Wisconsin Historical Society

Thankfully, styles have changed and modern bustles are simply fabric draped in a bustle style, almost exclusively reserved for wedding dress fashion.

Dress Closures

FOR MY WEDDING DRESS

Wedding *DRESS CLOSURES* are a necessary part of the function of your dress. Some serve only that purpose, as with the hook and eye or zipper closures, and others, such as corset laces and button and loop closures, double as embellishment details.

Often the bodice you choose will dictate the style of closure. This is often due to construction requirements but is sometimes just the whim of the designer.

There are four basic types of wedding dress closures: corset, buttons, hook and eyes, and zippers.

Corset Type Closure

CORSET CLOSURES typically lace up the back in a crisscross pattern. Some may have faux laces (laces that are only for show) and a side zipper. You may also find front lacing corsets as with two piece dresses that have corset tops and occasionally, a vintage or retro style corset bodice that laces on the side. There will be a same-fabric panel inset behind the laces so they can be adjusted to fit perfectly without exposing your skin.

When lacing your corset, be careful not to lace it too tightly. You may not feel it right away but a bodice that is too tightly tied will constrict your lungs. On this day, when emotions may be high, you don't need anything hampering your ability to breath.

Rosanna Haller

Button and Loop

BUTTON AND LOOP CLOSURES will generally run along the center back of a dress. They're usually very small (1/4") shank style buttons covered in self-same fabric which are placed through a braided loop on the opposite side of the dress. This closure requires buttons to be placed approximately 1/2" inch or less apart to maintain the integrity of the dress's shape. This area places a lot of stress on delicate dress fabrics, so if your buttons are reinforced, it's a good sign your dress is well made. Dresses will have enough working buttons to allow you to get into and out of the dress easily, usually extending to the hip, but may also have additional decorative non-working buttons that continue down the back-seam. If you have difficulty getting into a back buttoning dress, the opening is not wide enough for you. Ask your consultant to have the back seam opened further with additional buttons and loops added. This is an easy alteration.

Button and Holes Closure

BUTTON AND HOLE CLOSURES will generally run along the center back of a dress. They're usually very small (1/4") shank style decorative buttons, such as pearl or rhinestones, and fasten through a hole on the opposite side of the dress. This closure requires buttons to be placed approximately 1/2" inch or less apart to maintain the integrity of the dress's shape. This area places a lot of stress on delicate dress fabrics, so if your buttons and button holes are reinforced, it's a good sign your dress is well made. Dresses will have enough working buttons to allow you to get into and out of the dress easily, usually extending to the hip, but may also have additional decorative non-working buttons that continue down the back-seam.

Hook and Eye

HOOK AND EYE CLOSURES should use braided loops also (not metal eyes) that are much smaller than the button loop, allowing just enough of an opening to securely hold the hook at the opposite side of the center opening. Both button and loop and hook and eye closures will have an inner fabric guard to keep the closure from snagging or interfering with skin or undergarments.

Back Zipper Closure

BACK ZIPPER CLOSURES can either be the invisible type, sewn closely to the edge of the back opening so the zipper teeth don't show, or they can have a zipper guard which covers the zipper and hides it from the outside.

Side Zipper Closure

SIDE ZIPPER CLOSURES will have the same construction as back zippers but because they must be shorter, only coming as high as the armhole, they're more common to bustier or strapless style dresses. Both back and side zippers will have a hook and eye or hook and loop closure at the top finished edge of the dress.

Any opening that is not wide enough for you to get into easily should be altered. This is a simple matter of removing stitches from the center back seam and extending the closure. If you're looking at a dress with a zipper closure, the entire zipper will need to be removed and replaced with a longer one. This can be more costly. If the zipper does not extend at least to the hipbone, it's a sign the dress is not well made. If the dress is constructed well and still doesn't allow you easy access, consider another style.

Back Styles

FOR MY WEDDING DRESS

The front neckline of your wedding dress is one of the most important features in your dress because it compliments your facial shape, neck, shoulders, collarbone, and hair. The *BACK* of your dress is going to be seen a lot as well so the back neckline should be considered when choosing the overall style of your dress.

As with the rest of your dress, you want something that accentuates your best features and balances your shape. The neckline that literally frames your face in the front can have an equally dramatic impact from the back. Your shoulders, hair style, sleeves, and silhouette will all play a part in your decision.

A romantic, vintage, contemporary or architectural feel can define the dress's mood and you can be creative with your neckline opting to have one fabric element of your dress, such as tulle, lace, or illusion netting, incorporated as an inset into the back.

If you've chosen a strapless bustier bodice for your dress, the back must be constructed to a certain standard so the dress will maintain its structure. The back will be straight across or may be very slightly rounded or V-shaped. You won't need to choose a back neckline for this dress unless you want to incorporate illusion or lace at the top of the bodice.

If you love the look of an open backed dress (no back neckline), you have many options. You can have a dramatic Watteau draping from both shoulders. Abstract embellished cross straps add architectural flavor to an otherwise backless dress. A surplice draped front may end in a one shoulder open back with a length of drape down the back strap. Wide pinafore style straps, lengths of appliqué dangling loosely from a neckband, or a simple spaghetti string tie across the top back are dramatic options for a backless dress.

Many back necklines will be a *mirror image* of the front neckline. The back, in many cases, is dictated by the front such as with off shoulder, bateau, one shoulder, jewel, and portrait necklines. (See Which Neckline is Best for You).

First decide which feature is the most important to you - the back, the front, or the overall silhouette - then build your dress around that.

Corsets

CORSETS typically lace up the back in a crisscross pattern.
They can be laced with ribbons or cording. Some may have
faux laces and a side zipper. Most corsets will be a same-fabric
panel inset behind the laces so they can be adjusted to fit
perfectly without exposing your skin.

Draping

DRAPING at the back neckline will be loose unlike the sewn in "drape" which may be incorporated elsewhere on a dress. Drape which is sewn in to keep it in place will have volume, something which is not desirable at the back neckline. Fabric that has been simply tacked at the back like the Watteau will add dramatic fluidity and grace to the overall back shape.

Halter Back

HALTER neck wedding dresses have ties or a circle of some sort that goes around the neck to keep the bodice in place. By design, the halter is backless and the shoulders are bare. The back can have coverage which extends up to bra level or as low as waist level and even dipping scandalously beyond.

Keyhole Back

A **KEYHOLE** back will always have coverage at the sides and top of the back. This is what creates the keyhole which can be small or can extend from near the top of the dress to the waist for a dramatic almost fully open back. It can be oval, round, triangular, or diamond shaped and you may find some modern column dresses with an abstract shaped keyhole.

Queen Anne

The **QUEEN ANNE** neckline must have the high collar at the back. This is what dictates the style but you can opt to have the back of your dress open into a dramatic keyhole or keep it fully covered.

Scooped and V-Shaped

SCOOPED and *V-SHAPED* backs can range from very shallow to deep and dramatic, plunging all the way to the waist and beyond. The deeper back necklines almost always require some type of cross straps or lacing to hold the dress in place.

Simple Back

SIMPLE STYLES such as the **JEWEL, SQUARE, V,** or **SCOOP** necklines can also be reflected in the back neckline but this is not necessary. With these necklines, you may have the option to make the back and front necklines differ.

Headdresses and Veils

FOR MY WEDDING DRESS

HEADDRESSES and VEILS have traditionally had some religious or cultural significance. Head coverings were worn by both men and women as an expression of modesty or as decoration and there was a time when the length of a bride's veil signified her status, as did the fabric from which it was made.

Modern brides choose their headpieces as a matter of taste and the by the formality of their intended wedding. Whatever you choose, remember to proportionately balance your veil to your dress.

Most brides want their veil to match the color of the bridal dress. Since shades of white vary considerably, always put your dress and veil together to be sure they're a match.

There are three types of lighting - ambient (natural outdoor light), incandescent (regular household light bulbs), and fluorescent (the long bulbs used in offices). Regardless of the type of lighting that will be used at your venue, check the veil and dress in all three types of lighting, if possible. Many fabrics, especially specialty fabrics like those used in wedding apparel, have been surface treated and can change hue in different lighting.

When you're shopping for your veil, keep in mind that you may want to have it with you when you try out the hair style you'll be wearing the day of your wedding. Give yourself plenty of time to get it, especially if you're having it made. If you don't have your dress yet, ask for a swatch so you can compare color. Also decide on the style you want and whether or not you'll need a blusher and/or a reception headpiece.

There are many types of veils and headdresses, some of which are worn together, such as main and blusher veils or veils and wreaths or crowns. Veils and headpieces are listed here in alphabetical order.

Back Piece

A **BACK PIECE** can be a comb or a short gathered veil or both. Back pieces are attached at the back of the head, usually at the base of an up-do. They can consist of a short tulle spray, an embellished piece with stones, beads, pearls, or crystals, or a silk floral. Often tulle is combined with an ornament for an intricate display.

Birdcage

A *BIRDCAGE VEIL* is a short veil of wide loose net that sits at the top of the head and skims over the face. It never falls below the chin. You'll see birdcages attached to fascinators and small hats.

Blusher

BLUSHER VEILS cover all of the face and sometimes fall to the shoulder. They're designed to be worn during the ceremony and removed or flipped back after the pronunciation of the marriage. Some brides have them turned back after the processional by the person who is giving them away. They're usually worn as a second veil to a main veil.

Bubble

BUBBLE VEILS are designed to be worn at the crown of the head - the top back. The voluminous effect is achieved either by bundling or gathering tulle or by folding tulle back on itself to make it 'bubble'. The rest of the veil is usually on the shorter side and will cascade from the bubble down the back.

Bun

Bridal hair *BUNS* can be worn anywhere on the head - at the top, side, back, nape, or off-center. You'll see them round, twisted, French, or with tails. If you don't have long hair and would like the look of a bun, consider purchasing a hair piece. Buns are accented with combs, sprays, back pieces, bubbles, birdcages, crescents, and fascinators.

Butterfly

The **BUTTERFLY VEIL** is cut in a narrow oval with the sides pulled toward the back, causing it to cascade or drape over itself, giving the appearance of butterfly wings. Usually made of illusion netting and often trimmed with a lace or embroidered border, it can hit anywhere from shoulder to floor.

Cap

CAPS* or *JULIET CAPS are similar in shape to a baby's bonnet and fit closely to the crown of the head but do not cover any part of the ears or neck. They're made from bridal fabric or lace and can be embellished with stones, beads or embroidery, most often seen with a veil attached.

Combs, Clips, Pins

COMBS, CLIPS and **PINS** can be simple or elaborately designed
ornaments placed anywhere on the head. Often covered in
Swarovski crystals, they can be long, wide or round, simple or
dramatic and take on fluid shapes such as leaves and flowers
with soft metal sprays or even butterflies.

Crescent

CRESCENTS are a type of comb, shaped like a crescent or half-moon and embellished. They're typically worn around a bun or some other curve of the head.

Crown

A **CROWN** is a full circle that sits on top of the head. Usually made of metal and embellished with stones or beads, it can sit around a top bun and is sometimes worn to hold in place a fine mesh mantilla style veil with a front overhang. A lace crown (headband) might have an attached veil, pouf, or bubble at the back.

Fascinator

A *FASCINATOR* is a small hat or decorative hair ornament that's worn at the side of the head. It usually features feathers, flowers, beads, netting, or lace and is attached using a comb or hairclip. Fascinators can also be attached to headbands and veils, especially birdcages.

Flyaway

FLYAWAY veils consist of one or more layers of tulle that fall only to the shoulders, allowing the veil to fly away from the face.

Half Crown

A *HALF-CROWN* is a half circle, larger than a tiara in size and weight. It's made of metal and embellished with stones or pearls, and attaches to the hair with combs.

Headband

HEADBANDS follow the shape of the head and can be made of re-embroidered lace, fabric, or stones. Headbands can rest over the top of the head or circle the forehead and are often worn with a veil or pouf. They can be elaborately detailed or simple, narrow or wide, sometimes covering the entire curve of the forehead and the hairline.

Mantilla

MANTILLAS are made from a oval cut piece of lace or bridal tulle trimmed with lace and placed over the crown of the head. They traditionally fall to the fingertips or longer and are held in place by a high comb that stands straight up with the mantilla falling over it. Contemporary brides are wearing mantillas with a flat comb hidden by the veil or the bride's hair. The front curve of the veil can be left down over the forehead.

Pouf

A **POUF** is made from layers of folded tulle and is usually worn at the back of the head. It's often accompanied by a headband and sometimes a very short spray of tulle or a short veil.

Spray

A *SPRAY* is a type of comb headpiece made of feathers, crystals, flexible wire, beads, silk flowers or other embellishments, worn anywhere on the head and with or without a veil.

Tiara

A *TIARA* is a half circle that is lighter in weight and smaller in size than a half crown. It's placed on top of and stands away from the head rather than lying flat like a headband. It's made of metal embellished with jewels or pearls and is attached to the hair with combs.

V-band

A *V-BAND* lies across the forehead in a centralized V-shape with the two arms extending over the outer top of the head and attaching with combs. V-bands can be simple or dramatically embellished with stones, beads, and wire sprays.

Wreath

Bridal **WREATHS** sit centered on the crown of the head. They're usually made of natural materials such as flowers, leaves, twig sprays, even small fruits and silk flowers. They're sometimes embellished with ribbon streamers and are seen with or without an attached veil.

Raw Edge

RAW EDGE is not a type of veil but a type of a veil finish. Veils made of bridal netting will not fray or unravel. The cut edge of the netting is left as is, without rolling, stitching, trim, or binding of any kind.

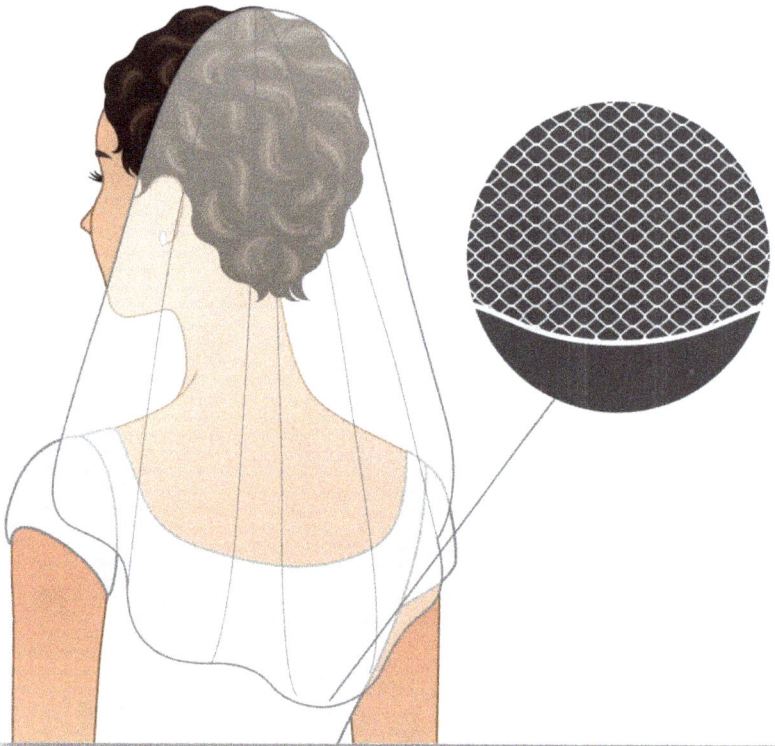

Rolled Edge

ROLLED EDGE is also another kind of veil finish and looks exactly what it sounds like. The raw or cut edge of the fabric is rolled through a small tube on the sewing foot as it's pulled across the machine plate, where it's stitched in place to create a smooth finish. This type of edging can be used with netting, or any type of veil fabric.

You can also find veils edges finished with fabric, embroidery, ribbons, or beads.

Veils Lengths

FOR MY WEDDING DRESS

The *LENGTH* of your *WEDDING VEIL* will be determined by the length of your gown and the formality of your wedding.

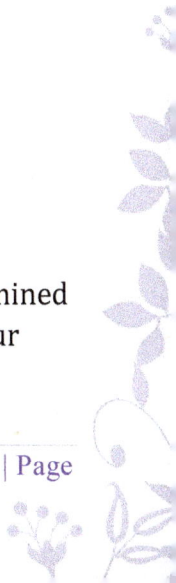

For example, a cathedral veil should only be worn with a cathedral length gown and only for formal weddings. At an informal wedding your veil will be shorter-if you decide to wear a veil at all. Though shown differently here, strictly for demonstration purposes, your veil should not extend past the length of your gown.

When you're shopping for your veil, keep in mind that the longer the veil, the more weight it will be to carry. Bring your veil with you when you are having your first meeting with your hair dresser to ensure that the hairstyle you desire leaves a way to fasten the veil without falling out or pulling on your neck.

Keep in mind that your veil may be of a different fabric and weight than the rest of your dress. Consider balancing fabric weights by choosing something lighter if your dress is heavy.

Shoulder Length Veil

SHOULDER LENGTH veils are single or double layered veils and are designed to end at the top of the shoulder. The top layer often doubles as a blusher.

Elbow Length Veil

ELBOW LENGTH veils measure about 30 inches and are single or double layered veils. The top layer often doubles as a blusher.

Fingertip Length Veil

FINGERTIP veils measure about 45 inches and will usually have several layers of tulle. They typically end at the bride's fingertips when her arms are down.

Knee Length Veil

KNEE LENGTH veils measure about 50 inches and are designed to end at the knee.

Ballet Length Veil

BALLET LENGTH veils, sometimes referred to as *PRINCESS LENGTH*, are about 54 inches in length, designed to fall to the calf.

Waltz Length Veil

WALTZ LENGTH veils typically hit at the mid-calf to the ankle, about 54-60 inches in length.

Floor Length Veil

FLOOR LENGTH veils are about 65 inches and are designed to just hit the floor.

Chapel Length Veil

CHAPEL LENGTH veils are the second longest type of veil, measuring 90 inches, long enough to reach the about two feet beyond the floor. They're typically removed after the ceremony and can be replaced with a smaller veil or headpiece.

Cathedral Length Veil

CATHEDRAL LENGTH veils are very long, measuring 126 inches in length. They were traditionally made of silk or embroidered satin, an impossibly heavy length of fabric, and are now usually made of fine netting. They're often worn with blushers, both of which are removed after the ceremony and replaced with a headpiece or shorter veil.

How to Shop for

MY WEDDING DRESS

It's important to know what to bring with you when shopping for your wedding dress. In the preliminary stages, you may feel as though you're only going to "look" but inevitably, we all end up "trying on", so carry a small tote filled with all your shopping essentials.

Create a Personal Resource Guide

The first thing that goes into your tote is a personal resource guide for reference. You can start a 3-ring binder or a simple spiral bound notebook to use as a reference guide. Use tabs to define categories such as "dress", "shoes", "veils or headpieces", "colors", "bridesmaid's dresses", "food", "centerpieces or flowers", "themes", "invitations", "honeymoon", and anything else you consider to be of importance*.

Search bridal magazines for style ideas and cut out pictures of dresses you like. Place these "tear sheets" into your reference guide. Write down the name and issue of the magazine and any other information about the dress: store, designer or manufacturer, price, color, etc. Leave enough room below each picture to write additional information or make notes while you're shopping.

NOTEPAD: Take a small notepad, one that fits easily into your hand. This is for taking notes on each picture. Each page, **front and back** is for one picture's notes. Page 1 - picture 1. Page 2 - picture 2. These will either be recopied into your reference book along with the pictures after you've uploaded and printed them, or you can simply tear out the page and paste it into your larger reference book.

CAMERA: You will most likely be carrying a phone or other device capable of taking pictures. Take pictures of each and every dress you like and make notes in your book. (If you're beginning by browsing online, most designers and manufacturers have store locators so you can see the dress in person.)

Mark the **store name** and a **description of the dress** such as:

Dress/picture #1 - Harry Winston sweetheart neck A-line with appliqué, satin, ecru, $169.

Dress/picture #6 - Vera Wang tiered silk organza, two-pc. bustier with straight across neckline, no train, comes with crinoline built-in, optic white, ecru, blush, or pearl, $469.

Dress/picture #11 - Maggie Sottero white spaghetti strap with V-neck, rhinestone back, champagne colored waistband, $3,500.

It's a good idea to hit one store at a time so you don't become overwhelmed. Be diligent about notating the dresses you like. That way, if you've looked at a lot of dresses, you'll be able to easily identify the ones in your pictures.

FRIENDS AND FAMILY: If you're the type of person who enjoys making decisions on your own or if you lose focus or are easily overwhelmed by the influence and opinions of others, do preliminary searches on your own.

If you enjoy the company and opinion of respected friends and family, take someone with you. It can be fun to shop this way.

If you're the type of person who has a poor self-image or cannot make decisions, take someone with you that you respect and trust to be honest with you in giving style advice such as an older sister.

SHOES: The dress hem is the least of the measurement concerns but wearing the right shoe can give you a better idea of how much you like the way a dress looks on you. Many stores have shoes available for trying on dresses but it's best to bring your own.

Wear the shoes you're most comfortable in, whether they're flats or heels. If you know the heel height you will most likely be wearing with your dress, carry them with you.

GLOVES: If you've already picked out your dress and you want to wear gloves, bring them to your fittings.

If you know for certain that you want to wear a certain length glove on your wedding day, bring them with you when you begin the process of looking for a dress. This will save you a lot of time by eliminating dresses that don't work with the gloves you've chosen.

UNDERGARMENTS: Bring the undergarments you would normally wear on a day to day basis.

Wear a *BRA* you're comfortable in, without padding unless you plan to wear padding on your wedding day.

Wear *PLAIN PANTIES* without embellishment, something that will lie flat and smooth against your body.

Wearing *PANTYHOSE* is optional. If this is something you wear often and you think you'll wear under your wedding dress, wear them while shopping.

COLORS: If you've already decided on a **color theme** (See Chapter "Choosing Wedding Colors") for your wedding, or even if you've narrowed it down to a few choices, take swatches with you. Carry them in a zippered case or stick them securely to the inside of your little notebook or for easy reference.

You'll need them for bridesmaid's dresses, sashes, stones, or flower embellishments built onto the dress, headpieces, or any other colorful element you might consider adding to your ensemble.

FLOWERS: You may already know what kind of flowers you want. You're flowers can be chosen to match your color theme so bringing your colors with you may be surprisingly helpful once you get started.

JEWELRY: If you know you'll be wearing a certain heirloom piece, carry it with you. Don't wear it all day while you're shopping if there's any chance it may get lost. Put it on each time you try on a dress and remove it before you leave the dressing room, replacing it in its box and in your tote.

HEADPIECE OR VEIL: Once you get to the point where you've decided on a dress, or at least a dress style, start looking for a headpiece or veil. When you get one, bring it with you on all future dress shopping trips and fittings.

If you have an heirloom headpiece or veil that you know you'll be wearing and you want to buy a dress based on the way it looks with your veil, bring it with you when you begin the process of trying on dresses.

BUSTLING: When you try on a dress with a train, ask to see how it will look bustled up. Some trains can only be bustled a certain way and you may dislike the silhouette once it's up.

Here are a few more helpful tips:

BUDGET: If you need to budget your dress, know what your limit is before beginning your search. Don't be discouraged if you can't find a dress within your price range right away. They're out there. It just takes time. (See Next Chapter: Seventeen ways to $ave money on your wedding dre$$)

CUSTOM OR COUTURE DRESSES : If you know you want to have a custom or couture dress made, start your search as early as up to two years before the date, if you have that much time. Talk to your designer of choice and he or she will give you a better idea of how long the design and construction process will take.

EXPAND YOUR SEARCH: If you're having difficulty finding the perfect dress, expand your search. Go to department stores and look at labels for designers' or manufacturers' names you may not have thought of. Get online and use key words "wedding dress designers" and find store locators. Go to trunk shows.

SECOND HAND DRESSES: Second hand dresses offer a great value if you're on a budget and you're lucky enough to find one you like. You can have sleeves shortened or removed, seams taken in up to two dress sizes, or let out some depending on how much fabric is within the seam allowance. Hems can be shortened or lengthened, embellishments can be added and some can be removed. You can even have an additional overlay or skirt layer added.

ASK QUESTIONS: Ask as many questions as you need to in order to find your dress or to make sure the wedding dress you've found is going to be perfect. If sales personnel appear annoyed, take a breather. Tell them you'd like to come back when you're feeling less overwhelmed.

RETURNS: If you see a second hand or department store dress you think will work but needs alterations, find out about the store's return policy. Once you get it home, take it to a qualified alterations seamstress. If she thinks there is something that won't work, you still have the option of returning the dress.

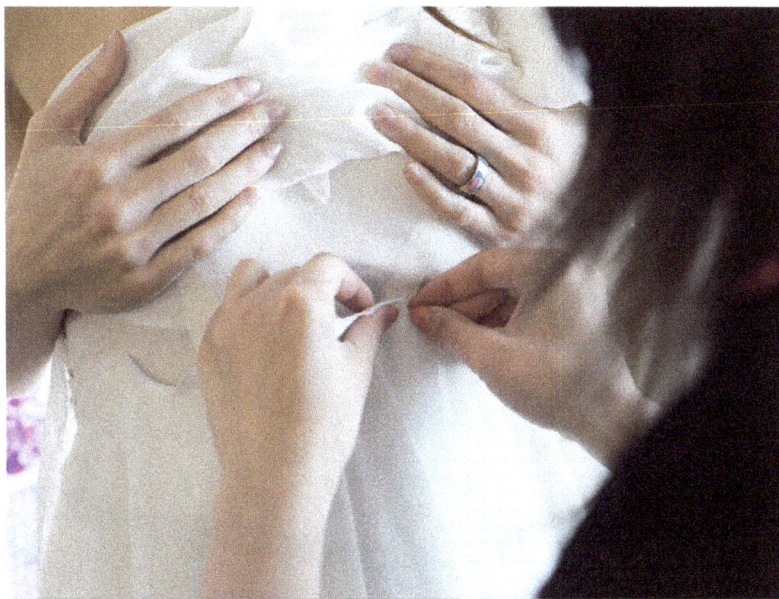

ALTERATIONS: Find someone who has experience in wedding dress alterations before you by a second hand dress. If they offer one, get a price list or get estimates and ask for references. You don't want to be stuck waiting for someone to finish altering your dress 2 days before the wedding.

FEES: Ask to have any **additional fees** explained, such as a **salon fee, consultant's fee, cleaning or pressing fee**, or anything else you don't understand. If you think a fee is an arbitrary "add on", *ask to have it removed*. Some salons will add fees as a matter of policy. It's best to ask about salon fees *before* you begin shopping in any particular store. That way there can be no surprises and if you don't want to pay fees, you can shop somewhere else.

As you start to build your personal resource guide*, you'll begin to see patterns emerge. You can eliminate certain items by simply removing the pages as you narrow down your choices. Soon you'll have the perfect book laid out before you to make concrete plans, bookings, appointments, and finalizations.

CONTRACTS: Ordering a wedding dress from a bridal salon will require you to sign a contract. Before you sign, take time to thoroughly read every detail. Be sure your name and phone number are correct. Specifically check to see that the order is for the **correct size, color, style number**, and **designer.** Double check the **measurements,** which will be sent to the manufacturer, **dress price**, and the expected **delivery date**. Check to see how many **fittings** are included in the quoted price and when your **first fitting** is scheduled. Check any **alteration charges**, and the required **deposit.** See that all figures add up to the **final price** on the contract, including **sales tax.** Make sure you receive a **copy of the contract** and a **credit card receipt** for your deposit if you pay by card.

17 Ways to $ave Money

ON A WEDDING DRE$$

People often spend exorbitant amounts of money on weddings and the bride's dress and accoutrements can account for as much as ten percent of that.

Some budget minded brides may be looking for ways to save money on their dress without sacrificing too much of the style and beauty they've always dreamed of for their wedding day.

The Top 17 Ways to Save Money on a Wedding Dress

Most brides tend to go to bridal salons for their dresses. These shops offer personal attention, but making you feel special comes at a price. So here are the top tips for cutting costs on the dress of your dreams:

1. AVOID TEMPTATION –This is the most important money saving tip. Tell your sales consultant what your budget is 20%-30% less than actual before she starts bringing out dresses. This way your entire final cost will be under your budget (including taxes and fees) and won't have your heart set on something outside your budget only to be disappointed or tempted to spend more than you know you should.

2. KEEP YOUR SILHOUETTE SIMPLE - The less fabric you have on your dress, the lower the price tag will be. A simple sheath will cost you several hundred dollars less than a multi layered full skirted princess silhouette. A shorter dress will also cost less than one with yards of train and layers of organza. Consider a high-low or cocktail length dress. Eliminate dresses with a lot of internal structure as these are more costly to make.

3. LOOK FOR AFFORDABLE DESIGNERS - Some designers specialize in more affordable dresses. Look for retailers who carry names like Maggie Sottero, Watters and Watters, or Allure Couture. These dresses will sell for anywhere from $500 to around $3,500 but you may find one on sale for less.

4. LOOK TO NATIONAL CHAINS - Instead of going to a bridal salon, forego all the special attention and try a bridal chain such as David's Bridal or Alfred Angelo. These retailers offer a wide variety of more affordable choices. The fabrics will be cheaper but you can find dresses from $300 to $1,400 or less if you catch a sale.

Chains will usually sell their own brands but Vera Wang's *White* line of dresses can now be found at chain retailers for between $600 and $1,400.

5. LIMIT EMBELLISHMENTS - Limiting the amount and type of embellishments on your gown can save you several hundred dollars. Beading, stones, and intricate lace details are time consuming to produce and are therefore costly to add to a dress.

For example, if you like lace, try something that has less detail and a more open design or go for an openwork appliqué instead. It's the shape of the dress that flatters, not the ornamentation.

6. GET TWO FOR ALMOST THE PRICE OF ONE - If you really want a longer dress and you'd like to have a shorter one for the reception, consider buying the shorter dress and having a professional add a long skirt that overlays the shorter one. This piece would be removed after the ceremony.

7. CHECK NON-BRIDAL RETAILERS - Everyone seems to be getting on board with bridal lines. Stores such as J. Crew, Ann Taylor, BHLDN (a new division of Urban Outfitters), and White House Black Market are selling dresses with simple silhouettes and the price points might just drive your decision. Many of these retailers' dresses are online exclusives so you won't be able to try them on without first buying them. Make sure you check the return policy carefully.

8. AS LONG AS IT'S WHITE - Look for non-bridal white dresses that can double as a wedding dress. You can check catalogs such as Boston Proper or Spiegel, boutiques, or upscale department stores - everyone sells white dresses for the holiday, vacation, spring, and summer seasons.

Shop online for a greater selection. If you key in "white dress" you'll find pages of them. Before you buy, be sure to check retailers' return policies and give yourself plenty of time to order, receive the dress, try it on, return it, and order a different one if you need to.

9. BORROW OR RENT - Borrowing a dress from a close friend or family member, or wearing one that has been in the family for generations, is a time honored tradition in many cultures. If you're superstitious, the dress should be borrowed only from someone who has a happy marriage.

Renting a dress will give you several style choices and this is an extremely thrifty way to go. Men rent their tuxedos so why not the bride? PreownedWeddingDresses.com, Woreitonce.com, or SellYourWeddingDress.com are a good place to start and unlike other pre-owned clothing, bridal dresses were truly only worn once.

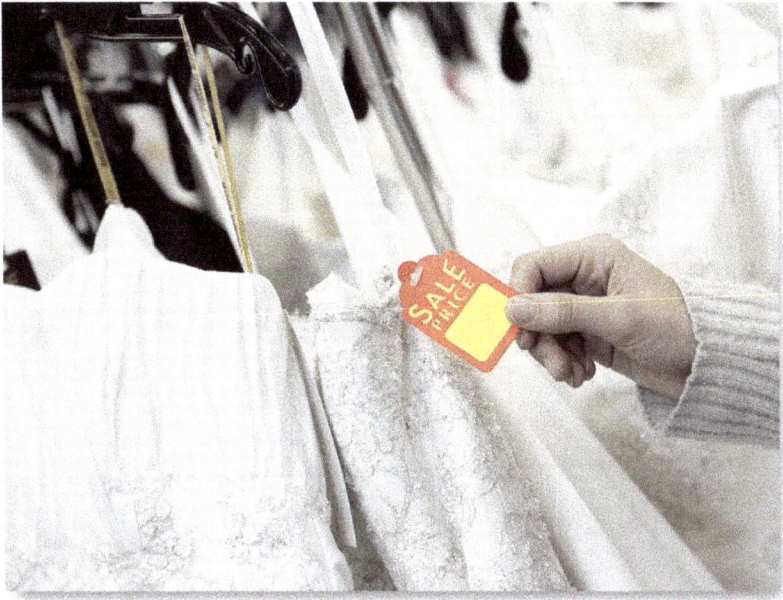

10. *THE RUNNING OF THE BRIDES* - You can find some incredible designer dresses at sample sales but be ready to put up a fight. These sales can be very frenzied because designers put up dresses for as much as 80% off retail. Be prepared to buy that day and you must pay in cash. Dresses may be soiled from being moved around so you'll need to figure cleaning costs into the price of your budget.

Call brick and mortar retailers and ask them when they have their bridal sales. Go in knowing exactly what you're looking for in terms of silhouette, length, and color. Remember, less on the dress means less on the price tag.

Off price department stores will hold sample sales a few times a year. These sales also offer discounts as much as 80% off the original retail. Check their return policy. Some may have an "all sales final" policy.

11. *LOCAL UPSCALE BOUTIQUES* - Check small boutiques in your area that specialize in dressier dresses. You can find prom and cocktail type dresses, or dresses that are marketed toward holiday and vacation. These dresses are usually priced in the $80-$200 range.

Very often local designer resale shops carry prom, cocktail, and wedding dresses. You may get lucky and find what you're looking for in your size. Even if you find a size larger, alterations may not add up to what you'd pay for a new dress.

12. *WATCH FOR HIDDEN FEES* - Some salons will add fees for service as a matter of policy. It's best to ask about salon fees before you begin shopping in any particular store. That way there can be no surprises and if you don't want to pay fees, you can shop somewhere else. Ask to have any additional fees explained, such as a salon fee, consultant's fee, cleaning or pressing fee, or anything else you don't understand. If you think a fee is an arbitrary "add on", ask to have it removed.

13. MAKE YOUR OWN - If you're thinking about making your own wedding dress be sure you know what you're doing. This is not something to be done lightly. There's a lot involved in getting a proper fit, working with many yards of material, and finishing touches. Many things can go wrong. Store bought patterns are often off in their measurements, you may not have purchased enough fabric, you may run out of time, and you may become overly stressed with all the other wedding preparations. When all is said and done, you may end up spending more money than you might have at some of the retailers mentioned above, so plan this carefully. However, if you feel confident in your skill level, or if you're working with a family member or friend who happens to be a professional, there may be no greater satisfaction than designing and creating your own wedding dress.

14. OPT FOR SYNTHETIC FABRICS - Let's face it. Some fabrics simply cost more than others. Natural materials are pricier than synthetics because it takes longer from beginning to end in the production stage of the fabric. Silk and cotton are more expensive than polyester and nylon. That doesn't mean you can't still have a fabulous dress. Technology has come such a long way in the production of synthetic fibers that often, we can't tell the difference between polyester satin and silk satin.

15. NEGOTIATE -Like other major purchases such as a house or car, wedding dresses are subject to price negotiations. If you fall in love with a dress that is a little out of your price range, be honest with the salesperson; see what kind of deal they can give you. Make an offer: if they accept it or counter-offer then great! If not, you can continue shopping. If you have it, ask if they'll take less for an all cash deal.

Negotiate on services. For example; professional pressing of a wedding gown could be up to $100. Try to negotiate this service into the price of the dress. Typically, bridal shops hire people at an hourly rate to steam press gowns on the hanger and it takes no more than two hours to press a dress properly. If they insist on a fee, negotiate $20-$40 for the service.

16. BUNDLE ITEMS -Even if you have to pay full price for your dress, you may still get a bargain on other wedding accessories if you buy them *all* at the same time from the same retailer. See if they offer discounts if you buy your wedding shoes with the gown, or if you order bridesmaid's dresses from them as well.

17. CHECK AND DOUBLE CHECK -Extra alterations or shipping will cost you more, so before you order a wedding gown, specifically check to see that the order is for the correct size, color, style number, and designer.

Double check the measurements, which will be sent to the manufacturer, dress price, and the expected delivery date. Check to see how many fittings are included in the quoted price and when your first fitting is scheduled.

Buying a dress on a budget takes initiative and creativity. Do your homework and use these tips to help find your dream wedding dress without breaking the bank.

How to Be Measured

Bridal dresses are the last vestige of utterly formal dress worn by modern women. The average girl, however, is not accustomed to wearing couture or custom tailored clothing, so it's important to know how to get measured. The first rule of thumb is:

FIND SOMEONE ELSE TO TAKE YOUR MEASUREMENTS!

Follow these guidelines and let someone do it for you. It's best to have a qualified consultant, seamstress, or tailor take your measurements and if you're ordering a dress from an online retailer, you'll need to have them ready*.

UNDERGARMENTS:

If you've already picked out your dress from a brick and mortar store, there will be someone there to take your measurements and you're likely to have more than one fitting. You'll know what the dress looks like and you'll be able to purchase the proper undergarments for it. Most bridal retailers sell foundation garments, slips, and crinolines but not bras.

When having your measurements taken, wear the same undergarments you'll wear on your wedding day. These will include bra, panties, slip, and any compression garments, such as a girdle or Spanx.

SHOES: You should be wearing shoes with the same heel height as your bridal shoes. If you're not sure what type of shoe you'll be wearing, don't worry about it. The hem of the dress is the least consideration of measurement and can be readily altered.

VEIL: If you're planning to wear a veil, have it with you at the final fitting. Veil length and fullness may also need to be slightly altered if there is a necessity to do so for balance and proportion.

MEASUREMENT POINTS: Consider the intricacies of taking a flat piece of fabric, marking and cutting it, then sewing it back together to fit precisely according to the individual's figure. Designers use specific points on the body as references. They're not random or haphazard. Tailors have been using them for hundreds of years to create miracles in clothing construction so if you want your dress to be well fitted, have accurate measurements taken.

Measurements should be taken using a paper or plastic dressmaker's tape and should be snug but not tight.

Measurements should be taken 2-3 hours *after* eating. For best results do not take measurements directly after eating.

There are numerous measurements for a dress and jacket. You will not need them all. The measurements you need will depend on the dress you choose, its neckline, sleeves, waist, and bodice style. Write them down and label them.

CIRCUMFERENCE: Circumference is taken around the body from point "A" back to point "A".

LENGTH: Length is measured vertically or horizontally from point "A" to point "B".

WAIST: Locate your natural waist by tying a string or ribbon around it. Don't suck your stomach in. The ribbon should be snug but not tight. If your natural waist is larger than your hips, the ribbon should sit about 1" above the navel. **You'll need this reference point to take further measurements.**

Dressmaker tapes are usually 4/8"-5/8" inches wide so find the center to mark an accurate waist.

Where the term *"SIDE SEAM"* is used, it refers to the imaginary vertical line at the side of the body centered between the front and back.

The term *"APEX"* refers to the bust point or nipple.

For all arm measurements, the arms should be down at your sides and relaxed unless otherwise indicated. Measure both arms and designate *L (LEFT) AND R (RIGHT).*

An *"ARC"* measurement is a half measurement. You will be measuring only one half of the body as indicated.

Measurements Checklist

Be sure to hold the tape flat and level, horizontal to the floor or vertical where indicated. Your dressmaker will know how and where to add ease so the dress is fitted but not skintight. If you're unsure, ask questions.

*If you would like a Ready-Made Measurement Checklist, visit **www.HelpMeFindaWeddingDress.com**

How to Measure the Neck Area

NECK CIRCUMFERENCE: Locate the depression between the collar bones at the front and below the neck. Measure around your neck at the top of this depression (base of the throat).

UPPER NECK: The circumference of your neck at the middle of the throat, midway between the base and the point where the neck meets the head.

NECK HEIGHT: Measure the distance vertically **Between** the neck circumference and upper neck circumference.

How to Measure the Bust Area

FULL BUST: Hold the tape horizontally across the nipples and measure your circumference.

UPPER BUST: With your arms down at your sides, hold the tape horizontally and snuggly at the underarm and measure your circumference.

UNDER BUST OR RIBCAGE: Hold the tape horizontally and snuggly under the breast and measure your circumference. Do not hold your breath.

EXPANDED RIBCAGE: If you're planning to wear a bustier style bodice, this measurement may be important. Take the under bust measurement again while taking a deep breath so that the ribcage is fully expanded.

BUST BRIDGE: Across the bust apex from side seam to side seam.

BUST TO WAIST: From the apex straight down to the waist.

BUST DEPTH: From the apex diagonally up to the outer tip of the shoulder.

BACK BUST: Across your back from side seam to side seam level with the bust bridge.

BUST RADIUS: From the bust point ending under the bust mound.

BUST SPAN OR CENTER BUST DISTANCE: The distance from nipple to nipple. Do not depress the center of the tape.

BUST LENGTH: From the apex straight up to the top of the shoulder.

How to Measure the Upper Torso

DART PLACEMENT: The distance from the center **front** waist outward to directly below the bust apex (princess line) **AND** from the center **back** waist to princess line.

SIDE LENGTH: From the waist straight up to a point 2" below the armpit crease.

CENTER FRONT LENGTH: From the center waist straight up over the bust bridge to the neck (base of the throat).

CENTER BACK LENGTH: From the center waist straight up to the base of the neck (the prominent bone).

SHOULDER SLOPE: From center front waist diagonally to the tip of the shoulder bone AND from the center back diagonally to the tip of the shoulder bone.

FULL LENGTH: From the waist straight up over the bust apex to the top of the shoulder, front AND back.

HALTER LINE: From the point where the side neck meets the shoulder diagonally down to the side seam, 2" below the armpit crease.

How to Measure the Shoulders

SHOULDER LENGTH: From the point where the neck meets the shoulder out to the tip of the shoulder bone.

UPPER BACK: Across the top of the back between the tips of the shoulder bones.

BACK: Snuggly under the arms from side seam to side seam.

How to Measure for a Corset

BUST TO CORSET TOP: Measure from the apex to the top of your desired corset.

SIDE WAIST TO CORSET TOP: Measure along the side from the waist straight up to the armpit within 1-2".

SIDE WAIST TO CORSET BOTTOM: From the waist straight down to the bottom of the desired corset. (For two piece dresses or dresses with Basque style waistlines where the bodice is a corset or bustier style and the waist falls below the natural waist).

CENTER FRONT FINISHED CORSET LENGTH: From the center of the waist straight down to where your desired corset will end. (If you have a larger stomach, please suck your stomach in *for this measurement only* and measure as vertically as possible).

CENTER BACK FINISHED CORSET LENGTH: From the center back waist along the spine to the desired corset top.

CENTER FRONT WAIST TO CORSET TOP: From the center front waist straight up to the desired top of the corset.

CENTER BACK WAIST TO CORSET TOP: From the center back waist to desired corset top.

How to Measure the Waist Area

WAIST: The circumference of your waist at the ribbon.

WAIST ARC: From the center **front** waist to the side seam **and** from the center **back** waist to the side seam.

How to Measure Arms

UNDERARM: From the top of the shoulder under and around the armpit and back to the top of the shoulder.

WRIST: Circumference at the wrist bone.

FOREARM: The circumference of your arm 2-3" below the elbow.

BICEP: The circumference at the fullest part.

UPPER ARM LENGTH: From the tip of the shoulder bone to the elbow.

ARM LENGTH STRAIGHT: With arms down at your sides, measure from the center tip of the shoulder bone straight down to the imaginary line at the wrist bone.

ELBOW: The circumference at the elbow slightly bent.

ARM LENGTH BENT: With arms bent at a 45 degree angle, measure from the back tip of the shoulder bone, around the back of the elbow to the pinkie side of the wrist bone.

How to Measure the Lower Body

FRONT LENGTH: From the neck circumference line straight down to the floor, barefooted **and** with bridal shoes.

WAIST TO FLOOR: At the center, from the waist straight down to the floor, without shoes, hoops or crinolines **and** with shoes, hoops and crinolines.

SIDE LENGTH: From side waist to floor with; **without** shoes.

BACK LENGTH: From the base of the neck straight down to the floor. Do not depress tape at body curves.

How to Measure the Hip Area

HIGH HIP: The circumference at the hipbone prominence, typically about 3" below the waist.

ABDOMEN ARC: From the center **front** waist to the side seam measuring at the high hip (3" below the waist) **and** from the center **back** waist to the side seam at the high hip. This is a half measurement.

LOW HIP: The circumference at the widest part of the hip, at the level of the crotch, being sure to hold the tape level.

HIP ARC: From the center **front** to the side seam along the low hip line AND from the center **back** to the side seam along the low hip line. This is a half measurement.

HIP DEPTH: From the center **front** waist to the low hip line AND from the center **back** waist to the low hip line.

WAIST TO FULL HIP: Place the tape 4-5" outside the navel and measure the distance from the waist to the low hip.

FRONT HIP: From side seam to side seam across the fullest part.

BACK HIP: From side seam to side seam across the fullest part.

Posture and Stance

It's important to stand as naturally as possible when having your measurements taken. It's common for people to try to stand erect when in front of a mirror but this will throw off the line of your dress. If your normal stance is slightly round-shouldered, your dress will be uncomfortable if it's measured while you're standing with your shoulders pulled back artificially. Everyone has a different body balance and stance, so *stay true to yours*.

Buying Online

There are many great online tailors, designers, and custom dressmakers. Each will vary somewhat in their measurement requirements and they should have a measurement form for you to fill out.

Try to avoid using size numbers as decision making criteria. A size number will only be a starting reference point. It's important to find out as much as you can about the retailer. If the site offers an online chat, take advantage of it and ask as many questions as you need to.

If you have no particular figure issues, you may do well with online customization but if you do have figure issues, you may fare better at a brick and mortar store where someone can properly assess your body balance.

Embellishments

FOR MY WEDDING DRESS

W hat is a wedding dress, if not its embellishments? It's important to select a dress cut that flatters you, but what will really turn your dress from a piece of fabric into a stylish wedding gown is the *EMBELLISHMENTS*.

Fabric Rosettes

FABRIC ROSETTES *are* realistic 3-dimensional flowers made from fabric can be attached to the dress to achieve a variety of looks. The size, shape, and color of the flowers drastically alters the visual impact of the flowers. Wear one large rosette on the shoulder of a vintage wedding dress, or a bunch of small rosettes on one side of the waistline for a modern, slimming effect.

Pearls

PEARLS are the most traditional stone for weddings, so there could hardly be anything more appropriate for embellishing your wedding dress. If you are planning to wear a pearl necklace or earrings, ornamenting your dress with pearls could tie the look together.

Beading

BEADING made of alternate materials such as glass or even plastic can also look great on a wedding gown. White beading adds a soft texture to your dress, but brides who want to be more daring could use colored beads to match their wedding colors. Beading is often stitched close together to create shapes like flowers, leaves, or other elements.

Crystals

CRYSTALS are polished and reflect light, and can be used on a wedding dress in a variety of sizes and combinations. Clear crystals add dimension to an all-white ensemble, and off-white or topaz-colored crystals add color without stealing the show. Colored crystals, because of their transparency, are a more reserved alternative to colored beading.

Gems

GEMS are any imitation crystals (usually rhinestones) that are used to ornament tulle fabrics on the dress bodice or veil to visually add "weight" or substance to an otherwise gauzy material. They are usually glued onto the veil in evenly-spaced intervals, but can also be applied in a pattern.

Sequins and Paillettes

SEQUINS are small, iridescent plastic discs sewed onto a dress to add texture and shine. These are common in figure skating and gymnastic costumes, but also can look fabulous when applied with finesse to portions of the wedding dress.

PAILLETTES are much larger than sequins, and hang from the dress by holes near the top of each disc. The paillettes move when the bride does, accenting her movement. Sequins, however, are firmly sewn in place on a dress.

Buttons

BUTTONS on a wedding dress, whether they are functional or simply decorative, give a wedding dress a lot of pizzazz. Buttons may be fabric-covered, uniquely-shaped, or even colored for more emphasis. Buttons are often seen going up the back of the wedding dress, even if they are purely ornamental.

Ribbons

Whether they are used as edging for the bottom hem of a skirt or as a contrasting sash with a lovely bow, *RIBBONS* add a sense of romance and femininity to a wedding gown. Sweet ribbons tied in the front of a wedding dress add a cute touch. A satin ribbon belt accented with dramatic beading and crystals is a look that's both trendy and romantic.

There are so many options for wedding dress embellishments it's hard to know where to begin. Regardless of the type or placement of the embellishments you choose, remember that embellishments should draw attention to your best features without overwhelming you or your dress.

Fabrics

FOR MY WEDDING DRESS

Wedding dress, veils, and wedding trim *FABRICS*, including accessories, are made of woven material. The weight of your fabric will depend on the thickness of the yarns used to weave it, the density of the weave, and any texture created during the weaving process.

There are many fabrics used in wedding dress construction from heavier fabrics used for the base construction of a gown to translucent fabrics which are layered over the skirt or sleeves to add fullness and depth.

So, there's a lot to consider: There is often confusion about fabric names. Yarns and weaves combine to make types of fabric. For example, **silk** is a fiber which is made into a thread or yarn, and it is also the generic name for a fabric. **Satin** is a weave. So a fabric using both would be a **silk satin** because it's made from silk and woven using a satin weave. You might see **polyester satin**.

Embellished weaves add to the confusion. For example, **brocade** is made by a technique that creates a pattern on a **twill** weave. If silk is used, you would have **silk brocade** but you might see **velvet brocade**, which is a **pile** weave or **silk satin backed velvet** created by weaving silk into a pile weave on the front and a satin weave on the back.

Keep in mind that your sleeves may be of a different fabric and weight than the rest of your dress. Think about your blusher and transitional headpiece as well as your main headpiece or veil. Consider balancing fabric weights by choosing something lighter if your dress is heavy.

The fabric used to make a dress drastically alters how it looks, feels, and moves.

Weaves and Fibers

PILE: A weave in which extra yarns are used and formed into loops. The loops are then left that way as with terrycloth or cut across the top as with velvet.

PLAIN: A simple weave using one horizontal and one vertical thread alternately crossing over and under.

SILK: A transparent fiber made from filaments of the silkworm cocoon. Silk is strong, elastic, and hygroscopic - it will absorb moisture if you perspire and still allow your skin to breath.

SATIN: A weave in which the face contains more threads to the inch than the fill, giving it a smooth finish and a high gloss. Better grades are made of silk.

TWILL: A weave in which the threads form lines running to the right or left, diagonally across the fabric. Additional fancy effects and ornamentation are obtained in pattern by introducing various twists and sizes in yarns.

Fabric and Finishes

BATISTE: a plain weave usually of cotton or linen and with various strengths: **Bastiste Claire** is very light and loosely woven; **Demiclaire** is of a stronger yarn and closer texture; **Batiste Holandee** is closely woven and has more body.

BENGALINE: Trade name for a ribbed or corded silk made from raw silk from Bengal, India.

BROCADE: Originally a rich and heavy silk fabric with flowers, foliage, figures, etc. woven in gold or silver core yarn or a color different from the foundation. Generally of taffeta, satin or twill foundation, but also velvet. The core yarn of bridal brocade will match the foundation.

BROCADED VELVET: Cut pile silk usually on a satin foundation and with a pattern of the brocade style; also velvet satin of any pattern.

CHARMEUSE: A very light silk satin faced fabric. It is dyed in the piece and given a very soft finish.

CHIFFON: French for rag; a very light, sheer, soft, silk fabric with a dull finish.

CREPE: Cotton or silk fabric of various weights, having a crinkly surface formed by the twist of yarns during weaving.

CREPE DE CHINE: A very light and fine opaque crepe.

CREPE GEORGETTE: A very light sheer piece dyed silk with a crepe surface and a dull finish.

DAMASK: A twill fabric. True damask (also called **double** and **reversible damask**) has both the ground and the large floral

Jacquard pattern woven in eight-leaf satin. **Single damask** is woven in five-leaf satin.

DOTTED SWISS: A thin and open weave of soft cotton muslin made with embroidered dot patterns.

DUCHESSE SATIN: A rich stout silk satin with a broad twilled back.

DUPIONI: A silk in which the double strand of two silk worms that have nested together is not separated, so that the yarn is uneven and irregular, causing characteristic slubs.

FAILLE: A soft ribbed silk fabric with wider ribs than grosgrain.

GAZAR: A crisp plain weave silk with a flat smooth texture.

GEORGETTE: (See crepe georgette).

GOSSAMER: An extremely light variety of gauze used for veils.

ILLUSION: Hexagonal open mesh; a very fine all silk tulle.

MATELASSÉ: A compound weave that has the appearance of being padded or quilted with ornamentation produced on a Jacquard loom and marked by raised floral or geometric designs.

MOIRÉ: A finish that creates a watered effect by passing ribbed fabrics between engraved cylinders which press the design into the face; the finish technique is best suited for ribbed fabrics although some smooth fabrics such as taffeta are treated this way.

MOIRÉ À POIS: Moiré silk woven with small satin dots on the face.

MOIRÉ RONDÉ: Moire with designs like the rings of a tree, all similar to each other; also called moiré francaise.

MOIRÉ METALLIQUE: A frosted watered effect on silk.

MOUSSELINE DE SOIE: Silk muslin, fine, sheer and lightweight with a crisp finish produced by sizing.

ORGANDIE: A plain woven, sheer, light-weight fabric with a smooth, crisp, clear finish created by mercerizing.

ORGANZA: Made with a fine silk yarn of 3-8 twisted filaments called organzine with different numbers of twists from left and right.

PANNÉ: Pile weave silk and wool fabric with a longer pile than velvet but shorter than plush; the pile is laid or pressed down creating characteristic light and dark reflection.

PEAU DE CYGNE: A stout silk fabric in a satin weave with a pebbled face and a glossy finish.

PEAU DE GANT: White silk damask.

PEAU DE SOIE: A stout, very soft silk dyed in the piece showing fine cross ribs on one or both sides.

PONGEE: Plain woven light or medium weight fabric made from wild silk, almost always their natural color of pale or dark ecru.

SATIN ROYAL: Double faced silk satin twill.

SHANTUNG: A soft but very heavy silk woven from wild silk and of natural color.

TAFFETA: A plain and closely woven very smooth silk fabric, stout and somewhat stiff with a luster, often used as a foundation for velvet or for the reverse side of satin. Modern taffeta is called ***chiffon taffeta***, a less stiff version made so by decreasing the thread count.

TULLE: Machine made net of silk or cotton used as is or further embroidered forming lace.

VELVET: A cut pile fabric of even depth made of silk. ***Double pile velvet*** has a ground of short pile with patterns formed of the longer pile (sometimes called ***cut velvet***).

VELVET ALENCON: A cut pile of lightweight French silk and cotton.

VENISE: Very fine damask with a pattern consisting of large flowers.

VOILE: A plain woven, light, sheer and clear fabric made of silk.

Laces and Trims

ALENCON: French needlepoint *lace* with the net resembling the Brussels point and having a raised outer edged of horsehair completely covered in cordonnet; also a lightweight French silk and cotton *cloth*.

APPLIQUÉ: Needlepoint sprigs applied to a machine made ground as in Brussels lace.

ARGENTELLA: White needlepoint lace similar to Alencon but with flat cordonnet and designs of very delicate patterns spread over a net ground having small dots at the corners.

BATTENBERG: Patterns formed with narrow tape joined together with various brides or threads connecting the parts of the pattern; *ribbon lace*.

BATTENBERG BRAID: Cotton or linen tape with picot edges used for lace.

BRUSSELS: Elaborate point lace with plaited threads in which outlines of flowers and veins of leaves are of raised cordonnet.

CHANTILLY: Lace of untwisted flat silk cordonnet woven onto a fine net ground and usually of delicate flowers.

CORDONNET: The silk yarn used to make cordonnet embroidery.

GUIPURE: Originally gold and silver lace also called parchment lace; laces with large patterns that stand in relief; also French for the thread for braid or passementerie.

PICOT: Loops along the edge of a lace pattern or the selvedge edge of fabric.

SCHIFFLI EMBROIDERY: Created on a Schiffli machine, the cross stitches are visible on both sides of the goods, showing the bobbin threads on the back of the embroidery.

SOUTACHE: Narrow rounded braid woven in a herringbone effect used for trimming.

VENETIAN EMBROIDERY: On a batiste foundation the patterns are outlined with buttonhole stitches and the ground is cut away with the parts connected with bars.

VENTAGLIO: Originally Burano lace from Burano, Italy; point lace of the finest quality with a net ground.

How to Choose Colors

FOR MY WEDDING

COLOR is visible light - an infinitesimal segment of energy waves out of the total spectrum of electromagnetic radiation - passed through a prism and refracted (bent) or reflected. All living things are affected by light and color is all around us but what we perceive is illusion - only the energy itself and how we're affected by it is real.

Colored sashes, trim, stones, headpieces, and shoes are all finding their way into the modern wedding. Aside from choosing your wedding's color theme simply by what you like, you may find it interesting to see why you're attracted to certain colors. Your flowers, your bridesmaids, your groomsmen, your invitations, your venue and even its lighting can all take part in displaying the colors that have the most meaning for you.

Color Symbolism

Here is a list of some common colors and the qualities society has assigned to them. Incorporate them for fun or to create the energy you perceive as being right for your wedding. The most important decision criteria is how colors makes *you* feel.

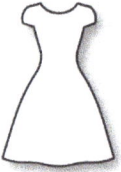

WHITE: the absence of color and associated with purity

GOLD: indicates wealth, joy, and luck

SILVER: Silver says "I can afford it, but prefer not to flaunt it." It represents wealth, glamour, sophistication, sleek, modern

CHAMPAGNE: is conservative, traditional, rich

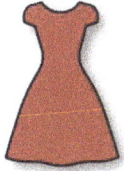

RED: indicates force, vigor, energy, and an outward direction to your life, prosperity; the preferred color in China for wedding dresses

BLUE: the color of the spirit, symbol of prayer and contemplation, cooperation, and tolerance

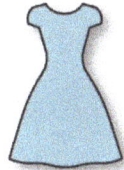

LIGHT BLUE: represents happiness, health, peace, tranquility, uplifting, fun-loving, harmony, truth, confidence, creativity, patience, calm, Cinderella and Happily-Ever-after

NAVY BLUE: represents preppy, loyalty, superiority, authority, order

PURPLE: associated with royalty, has an ennobling effect; said to endow the person wearing it with fortunate circumstances

LAVENDER: lighter and softer than royal purple; gives a feeling of benevolence

YELLOW: happiness, creativeness, inventiveness, courage, and strength of character

GREEN: the color of healing; the heart center; life vibrating into growth, joyful, gentle, and harmonious

ORANGE: associated with the seat of the soul, vital indicating thoughtfulness and consideration of others; optimism

PINK: a milder version of red with all the same indications but with a touch of softness

HOT PINK: represents energized, "Girl Power", love, friendship, abundance, lively, and playful

BLACK: a concentration of colors; reserved, authoritative; aside from being a fashion color, those who favor black often want to remain out of the limelight

BROWN: represents warmth and honesty in your marriage, also earth, nature, home, reliability, friendliness, steadfastness, outdoors, comfort, simplicity, and endurance

IVORY: indicates elegance, quiet, pleasantness, softness, and luster

GRAY: Neutral and unobtrusive; darker grays are more assertive while pale grays are unassuming

How to Choose Flowers

FOR MY WEDDING

You might use *FLOWERS* in your bridal bouquet, your centerpieces, your headpiece, inside the church or temple, in a lapel, or even as place setting adornments.

Flower symbolism has ancient roots in religion, spiritualism, mythology, and art.

Flowers are used in virtually every culture on the planet and they ritually follow us throughout our lives from birth, at holidays, as gifts, in marriage, to express what our words cannot, and through the end of our days.

Modern flower symbolism began in the Victorian era when feelings and emotions were not openly expressed, so a language based on flowers was developed. Their messages were clear and indisputable.

But why you are attracted to a certain type of flower may be an indicator of your personality. Coupled with the colors you like, you may discover a deeper side to yourself. Choosing flowers based on their symbolic attributes can make them more meaningful. Use this ancient art as a way of deepening the connection between the gesture of marrying and the relationship you intend for your new union.

The following list contains only those flowers that have a positive symbolic meaning. It does not include those with a negative symbolic meaning, such as the Bird's-foot Trefoil, which symbolically stands for revenge.

Remember that flower symbolism is not scientific in any way and has had superstition attached to it. If you love a flower and you find its meaning is not exactly what you had hoped, it's up to you to disregard this Victorian era fancy and choose what makes you feel wonderful!

ACACIA: secret love

ACANTHUS: art

AGRIMONY: thankfulness

ALMOND: promise

AMARANTH: immortal love

AMBROSIA: love is reciprocated

ANGREC: royalty

APPLE BLOSSOM: preference

ARBORVITAE: everlasting friendship

ARBUTUS: you're the only one I love

ARUM: ardor

ASPARAGUS FOLIAGE: fascination

ASTER: love, daintiness, trusting

AZALEA: temperance, passion, Chinese symbol of womanhood

BABY'S BREATH: innocence, pure of heart

BACHELOR BUTTON: single blessedness, celibacy

BALSAM: Ardent love

BAY WREATH: glory

BELLS OF IRELAND: luck

BERRIROSE: choose your destiny, I won't give up my promise, I'll love you forever

BUTTERCUP: riches

CAMELLIA JAPONICA: unpretending excellence

CAMPANULA: gratitude

CARNATION: white is innocence, pure love and faithfulness

CELANDINE: joys to come

CHERRY BLOSSOM: gentleness, kindness, wabi-sabi (in Japan)

CHINA ASTER: fidelity

COREOPSIS: always cheerful

CLOVE: undying love

DAFFODIL: respect, chivalry

DAHLIA: elegance and dignity

DAISY: innocence, loyal love, purity, faith, cheer, simplicity

DELPHINIUM: levity, fun, big-hearted, joy

FORGET-ME-NOT: true love

GARDENIA: you're lovely, sweet love, good luck

GLADIOLUS: honor, conviction

GORSE: love in all seasons

HEATHER: purple is beauty and admiration; white is protection

HELIOTROPE: devotion

HIBISCUS: rare beauty, delicate beauty

HONEYSUCKLE: devoted affection, bonds of love

IRIS: good news

JASMINE: unconditional eternal love (in Philippines)

LILAC: purple is first emotion of love; white is youthful innocence

LILY: white is purity; scarlet is high-souled aspirations

LILY OF THE VALLEY: sweetness, humility, trustworthy

LOTUS: purity, chastity, and eloquence

MAGNOLIA: love of nature

MALLOW: consumed by love

MOONFLOWER: dreaming of love

OATS: music

OLIVE: peace

ORCHID: refined beauty

OXEYE DAISY: patience

PEACH BLOSSOM: long life, generosity, bridal hope

PEAR BLOSSOM: lasting friendship

PEONY: honor (in China)

PHLOX: harmony, our souls are united, we think alike

PLUM BLOSSOM: beauty and longevity

PRIMROSE: eternal love

ROSE: red is true love; blue is love at first sight; white is innocence, virtue, purity; pink is grace; light pink is desire, joy of life, energy; burgundy is unconscious beauty; coral or orange is desire and passion; yellow is friendship; lavender or violet is love at first sight; red and white together is united; red and yellow together is joy, happiness and excitement; thornless is love at first sight

STRAW: united

TULIP: red is undying love; purple is forever love

VIOLET: blue is faithfulness

WITCH HAZEL: a magic spell

How to Choose Gems & Stones

FOR MY WEDDING

Diamonds are the traditional stone for engagement and wedding rings but many couples are using other *GEMS* and precious and semi-precious *STONES* as symbols of their commitment to each other, stones which have some depth of meaning within their relationship.

You may decide to choose a stone based on its symbolic meaning or, if you already have an heirloom piece, it can be fun to discover its symbolism in folklore.

Gems and Stones

AMETHYST (quartz) - calming influence, clarity, protection from intoxication

AQUAMARINE (beryl) - endows the wearer with foresight, courage, and happiness, increases intelligence, healing treatment for anxiety, calming

CARNELIAN - linked to the blood, energy, and power, quells envy and rage

CHALCEDONY - opens pathways where there's resistance

CHRYSOBERYL (cymophane) - has a stabilizing influence, protective, allowing forgiveness and a sense of self worth

CHRYSOPRASE (chalcedony) - a merry stone, a gift in times of joy

CITRINE (quartz) - the merchant's stone, engenders savings

DIAMOND (carbon) - the only gemstone composed of one pure element bonded with perfect symmetry making it the hardest natural substance known; represents clarity, power, incorruptibility, longevity, constancy, and good fortune

EMERALD (beryl) - represents spring and rebirth, protection at sea

GARNET (dodecahedron crystal system of minerals with nearly identical atomic structure) - thought to dissipate sadness and exhilarate the soul

HEMATITE (iron oxide) - connected in lore to Mars, the red god of war and invulnerability

JADE (jadeite; nephrite) - symbol of love and virtue; also transparency and openness

MOONSTONE (orthoclase fepar) - the stone of tenderness, opens the heart

ONYX (chalcedony) - associated with strong foundation, strength

OPAL - in ancient lore, the symbol of hope and purity or "child beautiful as love"

PERIDOT (gem quality olivine; silicate) - immovable, obstinate; also invulnerable, strength of character

QUARTZ OR ROCK CRYSTAL (silicon dioxide) - "stone of light", protection from danger

RUBY (corundum) - "the dearly loved stone", inspires love and strength of love, lifeblood, courage and bravery

SAPPHIRE (non-red variety of corundum) - 2nd hardest natural mineral; has a calming effect that facilitates prayer and meditation; also the Seal of Solomon

TIGER EYE (metamorphic rock quartz) - beneficial for health and spiritual well-being, helps achieve clarity

TOPAZ - in lore, said to dispel night terrors and cure cowardice, strengthen intellect and grant courage; creates its own light

TOURMALINE - provides insight and direction toward that which is good

TURQUOISE - in lore, believed to attract beneficial spirits; also healing, accuracy

Organic Materials Used in Jewelry

AMBER (fossilized tree resin) - a biogenic gemstone; represents opulent warmth and in lore, the strength of a tiger

AGATIZED BONE (fossilized bone with quartz cellular structure) - represents strength with beauty

BONE (the endoskeleton of vertebrates) - represents growth and strength, structure and protection

CORAL (marine animals) - represents relational symbiosis, family, dependency, singularity

IVORY (dentine from tusks or teeth) - represents security and home

JET OR LIGNITE (a product of the high pressure decomposition of wood over millions of years) - represents inner warmth

NACRE OR MOTHER OF PEARL (crystal formation of inner shell of some mollusks) - associated with protection against outside attack or criticism

PEARL (calcium carbonate) - a biogenic gemstone; represents layered theological metaphor, ancient wisdom

PALM WOOD (petrified palm trees from the Oligocene Epoch 20-40 million years ago) - represents wisdom strength, lasting relationships, connection to earth and nature.

Stones by Color

Many stones, such as opal, ruby, sapphire, garnet, beryl, topaz and others are found in a variety of colors. The following list shows some common and uncommon stones used in jewelry and may help you find the perfect stone.

GREEN: is said to represent money, prosperity, fertility, healing, and growth; the color of the earth, pacifying and refreshing, connected with nature

Emerald, chrome tourmaline, chrome diopside, peridot, chrysoprase, tsavorite, Chrysoberyl, bloodstone, alexandrite, jade, malachite, gaspeite, uvarovite drusy, sapphire, garnet, beryl, turquoise, green fire opal, spinel

BLUE/GREEN: is said to be purifying and calming; combines the cleansing action of green and the soothing action of blue; enhances creativity and helps connect to spirituality

> Aquamarine, turquoise, chrysocolla, variscite, topaz, amazonite, apatite, tourmaline, hematite

BLUE: (azure, cobalt, navy, indigo) will soothe emotions, promote truth, devotion, and sincerity, increase peace, faith, and creative expression, patience; symbolizes ocean, sleep, sky, and twilight; also wearing blue exclusively can make one tired or depressed

> Aquamarine, azurite, blue lace agate, boulder opal, chalcedony, lapis lazuli, sapphire, topaz, blue zircon, malachite, blue moonstone, sodalite, iolite, titanium drusy, tanzanite, hematite, sapphire

PURPLE: (heliotrope, lavender, lilac, magenta, mauve, mulberry, orchid, reddish blue, violet, wine) symbolizes power, spiritual goals, passion, leadership, respect, and wealth; strengthens generosity, inspires creativity and inner strength, enhances wisdom

> Amethyst, opalite, tanzanite, charoite, garnet, jasper, sugalite, sapphire, garnet, topaz, agate, lavender chalcedony, tourmaline, spinel

RED: (burgundy, cardinal, cherry, crimson, magenta maroon, scarlet, wine) will enhance energy, strength and courage; physical energy, strength, and protection; associated with blood, birth and intense emotion

> Garnet, pyrite drusy, ruby, coral, red dinosaur bone, jasper, Ammolite, sponge coral, sapphire, beryl, spinel, bloodstone, tourmaline, alexandrite, eudialyte

PINK: (coral, flesh, fuchsia, rose, mauve, salmon) enhances mental ability and soothes emotions, anger, and feelings of neglect, represents love, friendship, compassion, and relaxation; also childlike quality

> Rhodochrosite, quartz, rubelite, sapphire, topaz tourmaline, morganite, kunzite, garnet, calcite, spinel, mabe pearl, kona dolomite

ORANGE: (coral) will command attention and is the color of creativity, promotes ideas, is energetic and enthusiastic, and is thought to stimulate the appetite

> Fire opal, coral, zircon, citrine, Ammolite, sapphire, chalcedony, zircon, citrine, garnet, sunstone, amber, ametrine, carnelian, Chrysoberyl, topaz, jelly opal, agate, palm wood

YELLOW: (amber, canary, champagne, gold, lemon, mustard, ochre, saffron) enhances clarity, self-esteem, is cheerful and optimistic, signifies intellect, confidence, communication, eloquence and travel; symbolic of sun, grain, and thought

> Citrine, sapphire, amber, canyon jasper, quartz, palmwood, carnelian druzy, garnet, tiger's eye, berlyl, topaz, zircon, tourmaline, Ammolite

WHITE: (clear) is associated with protection, peace, and purification, it symbolized the moon, freshness, and cold

> Diamond, pearl, bone, moonstone, opal, sapphire, topaz, druzy, ammonite, beryl, zircon, rock crystal

BLACK: **(gray, charcoal, ebony, slate)** is associated with mystery and the great unknown, suppresses emotions, banishes and absorbs negativity

> Agate, pearl, psilomelaine, Chinese writing stone, Picasso marble, ammonite, palm wood, hematite (Alaska black diamond), sapphire, obsidian, jet, spinel, onyx, druzy, orthoceras

BROWN: **(copper, amber, auburn, beige, brick, bronze, chestnut, mahogany, rust, tan)** is earthy and grounding, stabilizing, and calming, enhances clarity and wisdom, and represents soil and fertility, friendliness, simplicity, health, and dependability

> Tiger eye, carnelian, citrine, topaz, sapphire, jasper, opal, agate, drusy, amber, Petoskey stone, llanite, palm wood, dinosaur bone, ammonite, baculite, smoky quartz, pietersite, zircon, tourmaline, Gibeon meteorite

You can have fun combining color and symbolism into your wedding but try not to take it all too seriously. Much of the "wisdom" of folklore is founded in superstition, with the exception of the real energy properties of spectrum color itself.

Wedding Party

DUTIES & PROCESSION ORDER

C hoosing your *MAID OF HONOR* and *BEST MAN*, those two people who will stand beside you throughout the process of planning your wedding, is something to which you should give some serious thought. Your *BRIDAL PARTY* will help throughout every phase of your wedding and, along with the rest of the bridal party, will see to it that things run smoothly.

If you accept an invitation to be part of a bridal party, understand that you're expected to pay for your entire ensemble unless the couple offers to pay for it.

The Bride's Maid of Honor (MOH)

THE MAID OF HONOR is usually a sister or best friend. She'll have a lot to do so if you have more than one obvious choice; select the person you feel has the energy and qualities necessary to fulfill the role. She'll need to troubleshoot emotional crisis, keep the bride laughing, and be a good listener. She'll be expected to:

♥ Lead the brigade of bridesmaids in their duties

♥ Go to fittings and make sure everyone gets their dresses and accessories

♥ Help the bride shop for the wedding dress

♥ Offer to address invitations

♥ Inform all guests of where the couple is registered for gifts

♥ Help the bride change for the honeymoon

♥ Assist in any planning decisions, as necessary

♥ Host or co-host a bridal shower

♥ Attend all pre-wedding parties

♥ Record all gifts received at parties, showers, or wedding (she can delegate some of this to a bridesmaid)

♥ Plan any bachelorette party

♥ Coordinate bridesmaids to the rehearsal including transportation and lodging

♥ Coordinate a bridal luncheon or breakfast

♥ Coordinate all bridesmaids to the ceremony and see that each has the correct bouquets

♥ Hold the groom's ring during the ceremony

♥ Arrange the bride's train and veil before the walk and after she reaches the alter

♥ Hold the bride's bouquet during the ceremony

♥ Sign the marriage license as a witness

♥ Stand next to the groom in the receiving line

♥ Take care of guests at the reception: tell them where to sit, where to put gifts and sign the guest book

♥ Collect gift envelopes (some couples make other arrangements such as a box at the gift table or a pouch carried by the bride)

♥ Get the bride's food from a buffet table, get her something to drink, instruct wait staff to keep her plate warm

♥ Dance with the best man during the first dance

♥ Assist the bride with bustling her dress

Bridesmaids

BRIDESMAIDS will pick up extra duties from the maid of honor, as necessary, and assist in all aspects of the wedding. Here's what's expected:

♥ Help with pre-wedding tasks such as writing invitations and coordinating responses along with the MOH

♥ Help with shopping for the bridal ensemble if necessary

♥ Co-host and pay for, along with the MOH, the bridal shower, luncheon or breakfast, and bachelorette parties

♥ Attend ceremony rehearsal and rehearsal dinner

♥ Run last minute errands for the bride

♥ Be on hand the day of the wedding to confirm flower arrivals and meet the Officiant

♥ Stand in the receiving line, if asked

♥ See to guests needs at the reception

♥ Dance with groomsman partner during the first dance

♥ Help the MOH with the train and bustling if asked

♥ Accompany the bride in visits to the restroom if asked

♥ Purchase a wedding gift with other members of the bridal party

♥ Provide emotional support

Junior Bridesmaid (typically 9-15 yrs. old)

JUNIOR BRIDESMAIDS will pick up extra duties as the bridesmaids do. Here's what's expected:

♥ Assist with shopping if asked, especially if she's a daughter or sister

♥ Help clean up after parties

♥ Pay for her entire ensemble

♥ Attend rehearsals and dinner

♥ Hand out programs, bubbles, rice, and confetti

♥ Walk down the aisle and stand at the alter

♥ Stand in the receiving line if asked

♥ If the junior bridesmaid is the bride's child, she may escort her down the aisle and stand with the bride at the altar, participate in vows

Flower Girl (typically not younger than 4 and up to 8 yrs. old)

Having a *FLOWER GIRL* is certainly optional but if you have a child you want to include, this is a nice way to do it.

♥ She follows the ring bearer or precedes the bride and scatters petals along the path; she can blow bubbles or carry a single flower

♥ She can pair up with the ring bearer or you can have two flower girls; younger children tend to follow each other's lead so they're less likely to lose focus

♥ Have her attend the bridal shower and parties so she's accustomed to the older bridesmaids

♥ Seat her parents at the front of the church

♥ Where children are concerned, expect anything - crying, dropping the flowers, lifting her dress, running away from the altar

Page (typically 6-9 yrs. old)

The *PAGE* is charged with carrying a long train. If you plan to wear a train of 12 feet or more, enlist the aid of two young pages to carry it during the walk in both directions. They should:

♥ Be old enough to understand the duties of carrying the train without tugging, pulling, or slacking

♥ Attend rehearsals

The Groom's Best Man

Even the toughest and the coolest of men may find themselves becoming unhinged at the prospect of getting married. Your *BEST MAN* is your valet, your confidant, and your set of shoulders to lean on.

If your best friend or brother accepts your invitation to be your best man, here's what's expected of him:

♥ Coordinate and lead all groomsmen in performing their expected duties

♥ Help choose the wedding attire and assist with renting or purchasing details

♥ Coordinate groomsmen's attire, particularly out-of-towners

♥ Organize and pay for a bachelor party, along with the other groomsmen, taking care to respect the wishes and faith of the groom

♥ Attend ceremony rehearsal and rehearsal dinner

♥ Assist the groom in dressing

♥ Attend to any last minute details or tasks requested by the groom

♥ Stand beside the groom at the alter

♥ Hold the bride's ring until vows are exchanged

♥ Stand next to the bride in the receiving line

♥ Sign the marriage license as a witness

♥ Give the Officiant a sealed envelope with his or her fee (paid by the groom), after the ceremony

♥ Enter the reception with the MOH when announced

♥ Dance with the MOH during the first dance

♥ Give the first toast to the bride and groom at the reception

♥ Collect gift envelopes along with the MOH unless other arrangements have been made

♥ Deposit gifts into the groom's bank account if asked or hold checks until they return from their honeymoon

♥ Decorate the "honeymoon vehicle" along with groomsmen and bridesmaids

♥ Assist the groom with packing for the honeymoon if asked

♥ Drive the couple to the wedding night hotel or airport, if necessary, after the reception, or hire a limo to do so

Groomsmen

GROOMSMEN will assist with any number of duties during the wedding planning. Like bridesmaids, you'll pay for your own wedding attire. Luckily, there's a good chance you'll be renting your tux. Here's what's expected:

♥ Coordinate with the best man in choosing and renting or purchasing your wedding attire and attend fittings and be sure you have all pieces needed when you make the final pickup

♥ Assist the best man in planning parties and attend all pre-wedding parties such as couples shower, bachelor party, and rehearsal dinner

♥ Assist guests and direct them to restroom facilities at the reception, and serve as usher at the church, if necessary

♥ Enter the reception, when announced, with the bridesmaid you escorted

♥ Dance with the bridesmaid you escorted during the first dance

♥ Assist the best man by alleviating any last minute tasks

♥ Purchase a gift for the couple along with the rest of the bridal party

♥ Help decorate the honeymoon getaway vehicle

Ushers (typically men 16 or older)

Though not part of the wedding party, *USHERS* are often enlisted to assist guests to their seats for the ceremony. As a rule of thumb, have one usher for each 40-50 guests. Here's what they'll do:

♥ Arrive at the ceremony site 45-60 minutes early

♥ Roll out the runner if it hasn't been done so by the church staff

♥ Escort guests to their seats before the ceremony, taking female guests by the arm

♥ Find out ahead of time which side of the church is designated for the bride and which for the groom and escort guests accordingly

♥ Seat the oldest woman first if several people arrive together

♥ Answer questions about the reception site, restroom facilities, and anything else pertinent to the wedding or the area such as hotels; direct the question to someone who can help if you don't know the answer

Ring Bearer (typically 4-8 yrs. old or 8-16 yrs. old)

If a *RING BEARER* is used, he's expected to be able to walk down the aisle with a pillow holding the rings, which are tied in place. Generally, fake rings are used but if the ring bearer is a bit older, you might let him carry the real rings.

It's generally less complicated to use fake rings and let the MOH and best man carry their respective rings. If you use fake rings and a young boy, the ring bearer will simply walk down the aisle and place the pillow at the officiant's feet or somewhere between him and where the couple will stand and then return to his seat in the front row.

It's very proper to use a teen ring bearer, typically 9-16 yrs. old, who will take the task seriously, creating a more formal or regal atmosphere. If this is the case, have an adult hold the pillow, with the real rings, until the ring bearer is ready to walk, and then hand it to him. He'll stand near the best man until the bride reaches the altar. When she's handed to the groom and they take their places, the ring bearer will then step behind the groom until asked for the rings.

He may also stand in the groomsmen's line until the rings are called and then walk behind the couple who will turn to the center and take the rings. Once the rings are removed from the pillow, he'll return to his place near the best man or at the end of the groomsmen's line.

Processional Order

The *PROCESSIONAL ORDER* may differ according to your religion or the type of wedding you're having such as a civil or military wedding. In general, once the bride has arrived, all guests are seated, and the scheduled time is nigh, here's the order in which the bridal party typically enters the processional:

OFFICIANT stands at the altar.

GROOM and *BEST MAN* enter from a side door and stand on the left side of the altar, to the officiant's left, facing the guests.

BRIDESMAIDS and *GROOMSMEN* proceed in pairs, with bridesmaids on the left, standing on the right side of the altar facing the guests.

The *MAID OF HONOR* proceeds next, alone, and takes her place directly to the officiant's right, facing the guests.

The *RING BEARER* walks alone and stands near or in front of the best man until the rings are brought to the altar, or if a child, places the rings at the altar and returns to his seat in the front row.

The *FLOWER GIRL* walks last, before the bride and stands near the maid of honor or returns to a seat in the front row.

The *BRIDE* and the *PERSON* who is giving her away walk last to the altar where she is handed to the groom. At this point the person giving her away returns to their seat.

The *BRIDE* will take her place on the left facing the Officiant and the groom on the right.

The *BEST MAN* and *GROOMSMEN* will take their places to the groom's right and the maid of honor and bridesmaids will stand to the bride's left, facing the Officiant.

Being a member of a bridal party comes with responsibility. It's important for all concerned that you consider your duties before accepting the invitation. In the end, though, this is a day to celebrate and have fun. Do what you're expected to do and above all, keep the bride and groom happy. Give them a shoulder to cry on, support when they need it, and dance, dance, dance!

Wedding Traditions

AND TRIVIA

When it comes to weddings, there are probably thousands of *TRADITIONS* and superstitions among the various cultures around the world. Here are some that are interesting, amusing, and just downright fascinating.

WHY SOMETHING OLD, NEW, BORROWED, AND BLUE?

"Something old, something new,

something borrowed, something blue,

and a silver sixpence in her shoe."

Probably the most familiar tradition, at least among Western cultures, the poem itself is English in origin. The tradition may be superstitious in nature but there's much to be said for the power of suggestion and how what we believe has an influence over our lives.

An *old* item such as a family heirloom that has been handed down through the generations, symbolizes continuity with past generations and family, a connection with the married female ancestors, and a continuance of the family line. Pieces of jewelry, a bride's mother's or grandmother's gown, a petticoat or veil, a small family bible, or even a picture in a locket are common old items

The *new* item represents hope for the future and an optimism regarding the bride's new life. It was important that a woman make a success of her marriage in all aspects of running a household, childbearing, and taking care of her husband. A wife who could also cook and had an income was thought to be of value beyond others.

A friend or family member who is happily married will allow the bride to *borrow* something of hers with the intention that her wedded experience will carry over to the new bride. It also served as a reminder that friends and family would be there to encourage and guide the new bride, especially in matters of the bedroom and household. Due to her lack of experience and age, a young girl would have been at a disadvantage for the tasks she would be asked to perform as a wife. The borrowed item could be a lace handkerchief, a bible, a stick pin, or a piece of jewelry.

Wearing blue is Christian in origin. Blue is thought to be the color of the spirit. In ancient Rome, the color *blue* was symbolic of love, modesty, purity, and fidelity which is why we always see Mary dressed in blue. Blue has long been connected to weddings and before the late 19th century, was a popular color for wedding gowns. Adding blue to the bouquet or headpiece, a blue stone in a piece of jewelry or blue crystal embellishment, a blue garter or hankie, even blue undergarments are all ways to add blue to the wedding ensemble.

It's unclear why a *silver sixpence* should be worn in the bride's *left* shoe, but the coin itself is said to bring wealth, or at least financial security and good management of household money. Some believe it also meant that the bride would always have a little money of her own 'tucked away' for a rainy day. Today, a dime or penny will do and many companies sell keepsake sixpences for weddings. The coin should be shiny and new, representing a bright future and honest money rather than 'dirty' money.

VEILS

There are many reasons why brides originally wore *veils* and many traditions surrounding them. In the Judeo-Christian-Islamic tradition, women wore veils to cover their hair as a sign of modesty and propriety especially when entering a holy place. Jewish brides wear veils to cover the divine light emanating from them. In pagan traditions, brides wore veils to hide them from evil spirits who might want to take away their happiness.

A veil covering the head and face is supposed to symbolize virginity. The Romans had their brides wear veils that covered the entire body, a symbol of chastity.

In arranged marriages (which were most marriages) the groom would not be allowed to see his bride until after the ceremony so a veil was used to conceal her until the contract was completed.

The lifting of the face veil and the kiss after the ceremony symbolizes the groom's right to take ownership of his property and gives him the right to enter into conjugal relations with his bride.

THE HONEYMOON

The Hindus believed honey to be one of the five elixirs of immortality. In the United States more than 5,000 years ago, several varieties of honey were packed for the journey to the afterlife. Cultures around the world have used honey for both medicinal and culinary purposes for thousands of years and some believe the honeybee itself to be sacred. Honey is mentioned in every major religious book as having some special significance.

Mead, which is made from water, malt, yeast, and fermented honey, was believed to be an aphrodisiac, enhancing virility and fertility. The bride and groom were to drink this honey wine for the cycle of one full moon, the time it took to fully consummate a marriage. It's believed that this tradition began in either Wales or Ireland sometime during the Middle Ages, anywhere from the 5th to the 15th century.

Another version of this superstition ho that the bride was to drink the wine for one month before the wedding to increase fertility and ensure a male child. Regardless of which is correct, the time period in which this took place - one moon cycle - became known as the *honey moon.*

THE BRIDAL PARTY

It's unclear exactly how the modern *bridal party* began but here are a few traditions that may have started it off.

It was believed that if several people, men and women, dressed exactly like the bride and groom or of a similar fine and extravagant nature, any evil spirits who came to undo the happiness of the new couple would be confused as to who were the real bride and groom.

Or it may have stemmed from an Anglo-Saxon tradition of a groom sending his knights to travel with the bride on her journey to the ceremony to ensure her safety and protect the valuable dowry she would be carrying.

GETTING SWEPT OFF YOUR FEET

Some marriages were not among two consenting adults. Others were forbidden by fathers who would not give a blessing to a girl if he did not approve of her choice of husband. The prospective groom would literally have to kidnap her, or *sweep her off her feet* and throw her onto a horse for a quick getaway. After some time, the family would consider her spoiled and the marriage would be 'kept'.

A BOOSTA

Broken English for '*a boost*' and meaning to improve, strengthen or encourage, or to cause something to increase.

A boost in the form of money is traditionally given to the bride in Italian weddings to help increase her ability to run a household. She carries a white pouch and guests place their *boost* into the pouch at the receiving line.

SWAPPING OF CROWNS

In Greek Orthodox Christian weddings, the couple's right hands are joined together. Following an ancient biblical tradition, both the bride and groom have crowns placed on their heads, which are then swapped three times. The crowns are a reminder that the couple may be called to sacrifice themselves for each other's well-being.

Diadems or brow bands were worn by the Persians, and then adopted by Constantine I. The corona radiata, like the crown worn by the Statue of Liberty, was worn by the Romans and was referred to as the chaplet studded with sunbeams.

BRIDE STANDS TO THE GROOM'S LEFT

This tradition began out of pure practicality. During many periods in history, men openly carried a sword, almost always on their right. Yes, even during their wedding ceremony. Naturally, the bride would have to stand at his left. Men often had to fight off those who would steal a bride and the groom would hold his woman with his left arm and fight leading with his right.

CARRYING THE BRIDE OVER THE THRESHOLD

For some reason, it was considered unlucky for the bride to step into her new home with her left foot first so, to prevent any stumbling or misstep, the groom carried her over the threshold.

THE RING FINGER

Jewelry was often given as a symbol of bonding and the giving of rings dates back several thousand years, though rings were not always worn on the fourth finger of the left hand. The eternal circle symbolized the eternal nature of the union and was commonly made of natural materials such as hemp, leather, bone, or ivory. Iron was used later and rarely was a ring of gold given.

The first known documentation of using rings as tokens of love goes to the Roman poet, Plautus, around 200 BC. Wedding rings were worn on the thumb, forefinger, middle finger or fourth finger and were known by their inscription which recorded the marriage contracts.

The ancient Romans believed the fourth finger on the left hand had a vein that connected directly to the heart. The vena amoris or vein of love has since been scientifically disproven, showing the veins in all fingers to be anatomically the same.

In Western culture, the Anglican Book of Common Prayer officially sealed the fourth finger of the left hand as the *wedding ring finger* (at least in Christian cultures) somewhere around 1789. You'll still find people wearing wedding rings on any finger since customs and preferences vary around the world.

OBJECTING

In Western wedding ceremonies, there is a brief moment when the officiate will ask if anyone objects to the union of these two people. The union of two people in Viking weddings (and many village weddings) was sanctioned by the village or community so the opportunity to object was given in case someone knew something that was not common knowledge among other members. An objection would have been considered a very serious gesture and an affront against the character of either the bride or groom.

BREAKING GLASSES

At a Jewish wedding, the *breaking of the glass* was traditionally done by the groom after the rings were given. Today, many couples break glasses together. The broken glass is a symbol of the promises of marriage which are irrevocable and permanent.

THE TUXEDO

Tuxedo Park in the village of Tuxedo Junction in New York State is an enclave that was established in the 1800s by a small group of wealthy land owners.

The coat actually originated with the Prince of Wales, later to become Edward VII. He wanted a coat that he could wear when no women were present, at informal affairs and gatherings where men were fond of smoking. The tailless dinner jacket was ordered to be of blue silk; a smoking jacket, he called it.

There were many American gentlemen who visited England often at that time and the Prince, who had begun wearing the new jacket, was allegedly spotted by one of the founders of Tuxedo Park, the tobacco heir, Griswold Lorillard. The coat style was introduced at the enclave's 1886 Autumn Ball. According to a local society page, "he arrived in a tailless dress coat and a waistcoat of scarlet satin".

The best qualities of this smoking jacket were combined with the structure of the formal tailcoat. The shawl collar and softer fabrics were removed and replaced with a lapel and the more finished fabric of the tailcoat, thus making it more acceptable for informal evening wear.

According to one founding member of the Tuxedo Park club, "some of the members wore it one evening at a bachelor dinner at Delmonico's in the city (referring to Manhattan). This was the only place, at that time, where gentlemen dined in public. When other men asked what the members were wearing, they were told that this is what they wear for dinner up in Tuxedo." And so the *tuxedo* got its name.

More Wedding Trivia

THE PROPOSAL was an offer made between families for an 'intent to reserve' a boy and girl for marriage. If the proposal was accepted, a contract was made.

In the 1890s, this gathering, meant to strengthen ties between the bride and her female friends, was accompanied by small gifts to the bride. They were placed in a parasol which the bride then opened above her head and the *bridal shower* rained down upon her.

In ancient Sparta, men would gather around the groom to celebrate his finding a suitable bride. The *bachelor party*, made up of his military comrades and male family, would feast and toast his good fortune.

GIVING THE BRIDE AWAY is a misnomer. Arranging a marriage was common at one time and is still in practice today in some parts of the world. A groom was expected to give some sort of property to the bride's father in exchange for her hand in marriage.

The newly married couple was considered to be lucky so anything they touched would have held that luck. Small tokens or *wedding favors* were given to each guest, something to take home with them that would bring them luck throughout the year. The same luck was thought to be part of the *garter* and *bouquet* which is why they're tossed to the crowd. The idea was that the first to touch these objects would have luck shine upon them and they would soon marry.

Since women were considered property, she was expected to *change her surname* from that of her father to that of the new owner, her husband.

Grains signified abundance, prosperity, and the fertility of the ground. *Throwing rice* (or wheat) at the couple was meant as a wish for good fortune and many children.

"YOU MAY KISS THE BRIDE". Kissing was a legal bond that sealed all contracts.

Why White? A Brief History of Today's Wedding Dress

Wedding attire may vary among cultures but it's well known that almost all brides want to wear something very special for their wedding day. Though countries have traditional garb rooted in their own histories, most Western wedding traditions have their origins in ancient Rome. But where did the idea of the "wedding dress" begin?

The bride's appearance reflected directly on her family, so the clothes she wore at her wedding (which was usually arranged) were the best the family had. Rich colors, furs, velvets, and silks were the expected norm and no expense was spared (a custom that still holds today).

Even for the lower classes, the wedding was still a high occasion and they dressed as formally as their circumstances allowed. They used humbler fabrics but the styles of the nobility were copied as much as possible.

Styles were in keeping with the current mode so in the 1300s, for example, the wedding garment went from being a loose fitting tunic style to a close fitting coat with long tight sleeves. It was laced in the front or back and the front had a full slit to "show off" the under dress which also carried a train.

But the wedding dress as we know it today is a fairly modern phenomenon. Dresses don't follow any particular type of fashion or trend. There's an "anything goes" eclectic blend of sensibility and the bride has the option to wear whatever suits her fancy.

In the 18th century and earlier, however, weddings were about political alliances. Even among the lower classes they were about the transfer of wealth and substance, not about romance. One of the most obvious symbols of wealth was the clothes people wore. Textiles and the garments worn by society were made of richer fabrics with more elaborate weaves with the rarer colors indicating a higher status of wealth. Before bleaching techniques were perfected, white was very difficult to achieve and also to maintain.

Though England's Queen Victoria is most often credited with popularizing the white wedding dress, there were other precedents.

The daughter of England's Henry IV, Princess Phillipa, wore a tunic and mantle of white satin at her marriage in 1406.

Anne of Brittany wore white at her marriage in 1499.

Marguerite of Valois wore a white ermine dress and a blue coat with a five foot train in 1527.

Elizabeth of Bohemia and her maids wore white robes with silver lace at her marriage in 1613. Her sleeves and long train were covered in diamonds, paid for by her father, James I of England and Scotland.

Prior to her reign (1837-1901), most brides continued to wear blue, the symbol of purity as set forth by the Roman Catholic Church. Often the veil was the most elaborate part of the outfit with the dress being kept simple in design and not heavily embellished.

In 1840, Victoria, who was by now Queen of England, married Prince Albert of Saxe-Coburg. Victoria wanted to make a statement. She was a head of state. Because all the others who wore something white before her were princesses, she wanted to set herself apart. No one had worn a completely white ensemble before. Her dress was plain cream silk satin (considered white) and her veil was cream lace. When a picture of her in her dress was published, white became the dress in demand by high society brides.

Victoria's daughters, the princesses Alice and Alexandra, carried on the tradition by wearing white at their marriages in 1858 and 1863.

For the rest of the century, white continued to gain popularity and soon became the modern symbol of purity and innocence. But for many working class brides, marrying in a lavish gown one would never wear again was an extravagance they could not justify. Many continued to wear blues, greens, and even black if they were marrying a widower.

With the Industrial Revolution of the 19th century came the department store and with it came greater accessibility of fabrics and designs. Styles continued to change through the war years, prohibition, and the Great Depression. The 20th century saw the beginning of synthetic fabrics and the white dress was no longer only the domain of the very wealthy.

In many cases, the white dress of today is worn more out of tradition than virtue. With the rise of the global community, women are marrying later and embracing their own individual looks. But although dresses and styles may be more eclectic than ever, Western culture continues to embrace the white wedding dress and though we have seen shades of gold and silver and other accent colors being added, there are no signs that this love affair will end any time soon.

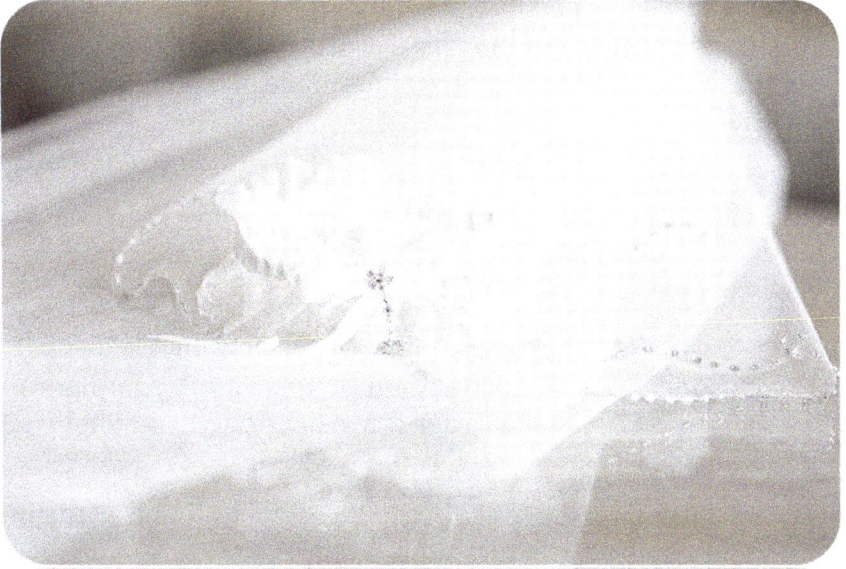

Glossary

OF WEDDING TERMS

There are many new terms you'll hear when you're looking to find a wedding dress. Different names of Fabrics, Laces, Trims, and terms such as "Couture". Use this *GLOSSARY* to reference these new terms.

COUTURE: Defines a garment whose pattern has been designed for one specific individual. It's made from scratch. Couture dresses must be completely hand-made and will likely outlast your lifetime.

Couture is governed by the rules of the Chambré Syndicale de la Haute Couture but the term "couture" is also used loosely to describe any garment that is hand-made of a high quality and standard.

CUSTOM MADE: Defines a garment that is constructed for a specific individual and can be sewn in part on a machine. The pattern is often individually made but can be made from pre-existing pattern pieces know as blocks.

MADE TO ORDER (MTO): Defines a garment that is made from an existing pattern which is then customized to your figure specifications. Made to Order can also be partly or wholly hand-made.

READY-TO-WEAR (RTW): Defines a garment that is made in standardized sizes in numerous quantities.

OFF-THE-RACK: Defines a garment that comes from "available stock".

ALTERED: A dress that has been taken apart at certain seams, according to the client's figure specifications, and sewn back together so as to create a better fit. Almost any dress can be altered up to two sizes. When going larger, there needs to be enough fabric to let out seams. When going smaller, there should be little or no distortion is the style lines.

Author:

Rosanna Haller

Wedding coordinator, Rosanna Haller guides and empowers bewildered brides to become savvy shoppers. Brides find their perfect wedding gown for their personality and body type by using the process:

B♥R♥I♥D♥E♥S

Rosanna, who graduated Magna Cum Laude from the Fashion Institute of Design and Merchandising (FIDM), realized an enormous lack of information for brides who needed to find their perfect wedding gown for their personality, body type, and event type. She created The B♥R♥I♥D♥E♥S Wedding Guide; Help Me Find a Wedding Dress. Visit: www.HelpMeFindAWeddingDress.com

Illustrator:

Naoko Matsunaga of Naoko Art

www.naokoart.com

A professional designer, patternmaker, and illustrator in the fashion industry for more than 8 years Naoko studied art and fashion in Tokyo at Esmod Japan. After graduating, she parlayed her previous illustration experience into a full time career as an independent illustrator.

Picture Credit:

Page i, © B.R.I.D.E.S. Guide, based on illustration by bikeriderlondon, Shutterstock.com

Page iii, © B.R.I.D.E.S. Guide, based on illustration by bikeriderlondon, Shutterstock.com

Page 2, © DmZ, Shutterstock.com

Page 3, © artida, Shutterstock.com

Page 4, © kireewong foto, Shutterstock.com

Page 5, © B.R.I.D.E.S. Guide

Page 6, © oliveromg, Shutterstock.com

Page 8, © Hugo Felix, Shutterstock.com

Page 9, © Michal Kowalski, Shutterstock.com

Page 10, © violetblue, Shutterstock.com

Page 12, © Eduard Derule, Shutterstock.com

Page 13, © artida, Shutterstock.com

Page 15, © Subbotina Anna, Shutterstock.com

Page 17, © Kiselev Andrey Valerevich, Shutterstock.com

Page 18, © Eduard Derule, Shutterstock.com

Page 19, © artida, Shutterstock.com

Page 20, © Mila Supinskaya, Shutterstock.com

Page 21, © kao, Shutterstock.com

Page 22, © Subbotina Anna, Shutterstock.com

Page 23, © freya photographer, Shutterstock.com

Page 24, © Subbotina Anna, Shutterstock.com

Page 25, © ChameleonsEye, Shutterstock.com

Page 26, © Dmitriy Raykin, Shutterstock.com

Page 27, © Subbotina Anna, Shutterstock.com

Page 28, © Olga Ekaterincheva, Shutterstock.com

Page 29, © Kiselev Andrey Valerevich, Shutterstock.com

Page 30, © freya photographer, Shutterstock.com

Page 31, © Subbotina Anna, Shutterstock.com

Page 32, © Elena Kharichkina, Shutterstock.com

Page 33, © Subbotina Anna, Shutterstock.com

Page 34, © Subbotina Anna, Shutterstock.com

Page 35, © Alena Ozerova, Shutterstock.com

Page 36, © Kiselev Andrey Valerevich, Shutterstock.com

Page 37, © Apple Eyes Studio, Shutterstock.com

Page 38, © Alex Andrei, Shutterstock.com

Page 39, © Kisialiou Yury, Shutterstock.com

Page 40, © Tracey Patterson, Shutterstock.com

Page 41, © Iryna Prokofieva, Shutterstock.com

Page 42, © MNStudio, Shutterstock.com

Page 43, © B.R.I.D.E.S. Guide

Page 44, © Lestertair, Shutterstock.com

Page 45, © Joshua Rainey Photogrpahy, Shutterstock.com

Page 46, © Mike Flippo, Shutterstock.com

Page 47, © hrk422, Shutterstock.com

Page 49, © Photobac, Shutterstock.com

Page 51, © bride6, Shutterstock.com

Page 52, © Eduard Derule, Shutterstock.com

Page 53, © Irina Fedotova, Shutterstock.com

Page 54, © NatUlrich, Shutterstock.com

Pages 55-261 (inclusive), © B.R.I.D.E.S. Guide

Page 263, © B.R.I.D.E.S. Guide, based on photo by bikeriderlondon, Shutterstock.com

Page 264, © # 137223662, Shutterstock.com

Page 265, © ARZTSAMUI, Shutterstock.com

Page 267, © milaphotos, Shutterstock.com

Page 268, © D7INAMI7S, Shutterstock.com

Page 270, © Maxim Blinkov, Shutterstock.com

Page 271, © Petr Malyshev, Shutterstock.com

Page 272, © lenetstan, Shutterstock.com

Page 273, © B.R.I.D.E.S. Guide

Page 275, © Johanna Goodyear, Shutterstock.com

Page 277, © bikeriderlondon, Shutterstock.com

Page 278, © Forewer, Shutterstock.com

Page 280, © vnlit, Shutterstock.com

Page 281, © B.R.I.D.E.S. Guide, based on image by Roman Sigaev, Shuttertock.com

Page 282, © magnola, Shutterstock.com

Page 285, © Sergey Novikov, Shutterstock.com

Page 286, © Sergey Novikov, Shutterstock.com

Page 287, © Sergey Novikov, Shutterstock.com

Page 288, © Sergey Novikov, Shutterstock.com

Page 289, © Sergey Novikov, Shutterstock.com

Page 290, © Sergey Novikov, Shutterstock.com

Page 290, © Evru, Shutterstock.com

Page 293, © Sergey Novikov, Shutterstock.com

Page 294, © Sergey Novikov, Shutterstock.com

Page 296, © withGod, Shutterstock.com

Page 299, © Natalia Melychuk, Shutterstock.com

Page 300, © Nneirda, Shutterstock.com

Page 301, © AlexussK, Shutterstock.com

Page 302, © Dasha Petrenko, Shutterstock.com

Page 303, © Ekaterina Pokrovskaya, Shutterstock.com

Page 304, © Surkov Vladimir, Shutterstock.com

Page 305, © Kotin, Shutterstock.com

Page 306, © Surkov Vladimir, Shutterstock.com

Page 307, © mellis, Shutterstock.com

Page 309, © alicedanie, Shutterstock.com

Pages 317-322 (inclusive), © B.R.I.D.E.S. Guide

Page 323, © B.R.I.D.E.S. Guide

Page 329, © B.R.I.D.E.S. Guide

Page 337, © B.R.I.D.E.S. Guide

Page 347, © Irina_QQQ's, Shutterstock.com

Page 362, © Lana K, Shutterstock.com

Notes:

Notes:

Notes:

Notes:

Notes:

Notes:

Notes:

Notes:

Notes:

Notes:

www.ingramcontent.com/pod-product-compliance
Lightning Source LLC
Chambersburg PA
CBHW072045020426
42334CB00017B/1393